CW01511723

92

FROM MARX TO THE MARKET

FROM MARX TO THE MARKET:

SOCIALISM IN SEARCH OF AN ECONOMIC SYSTEM

Włodzimierz Brus
and
Kazimierz Laski

CLARENDON PRESS · OXFORD

Oxford University Press, Walton Street, Oxford OX2 6DP

Oxford New York Toronto
Delhi Bombay Calcutta Madras Karachi
Petaling Jaya Singapore Hong Kong Tokyo
Nairobi Dar es Salaam Cape Town
Melbourne Auckland

and associated companies in
Berlin Ibadan

Oxford is a trade mark of Oxford University Press

Published in the United States
by Oxford University Press, New York

© W. Brus and K. Laski 1989

First published 1989
Hardback reprinted 1991
New in paperback issued 1991

Paperback reprinted 1992

British Library Cataloguing in Publication Data
Brus, Wlodzimierz
From Marx to the market in search of an
economic system.
1. Communist countries. Economic policies
I Title   II. Laski, Kazimierz
330.9171'7
ISBN 0-19-823302-7
ISBN 0-19-828399-7 (Pbk)

Library of Congress Cataloging in Publication Data
Brus, Wlodzimierz
From Marx to the market: socialism in search of an economic system/
Wlodzimierz Brus and Kazimierz Laski.
Bibliography: p.
Includes index
1. Mixed economy.   2. Socialism.   3. Hungary—Economic
policy—1968-   4. Yugoslavia—Economic policy—1945-   I. Laski,
Kazimierz.   II. Title.
HB90.B78   1989   335.4—dc20   89-15974
ISBN 0-19-823302-7
ISBN 0-19-828399-7 (Pbk)

Printed in Great Britain by
Biddles Ltd.
Guildford and King's Lynn

Preface

We have been prompted to produce this book by a strong desire to reappraise our stand with regard to socialism as an economic system. Each of us in his own way had been in the past fascinated by the apparent ability of a socialist economy to overcome the irrationality of capitalism on a macroscale—the coexistence of excess capital, excess labour, and unsatisfied wants. At first the possibility of combining this ability with microeconomic efficiency seemed to be only a question of time, and would allow the perfection of planning techniques and the full development of cooperative behaviour by the new socialist beings. When the dismal experience of the command system in our native Poland and throughout the Soviet bloc made us look for the prospect of reform after the mid 1950s, we still strove for a compromise solution, blending macroeconomic central planning with autonomy of market-regulated state enterprise. Subsequent continuous and careful observation of the tortuous reform process, including the Chinese one over the last ten years, brought us to the conclusion—not particularly original nowadays—that such a compromise was conceptually unviable, and that if marketization is the right direction of change it must be pursued consistently. In practice a tendency towards fully fledged market socialism began to manifest itself in the 1980s in most countries committed to economic reform.

The trouble with these conclusions and observed practical tendencies was, however, that they could not easily be accommodated within the same framework of socialist economics. They demanded—so we felt—a reconsideration of a number of fundamental issues against the background of a general survey of the main stages and aspects of the evolution of the socialist economic system. The results of this reconsideration are presented here—in a book the size of which conceals rather than reveals the amount of time and toil put into it by the authors. But this, of course, does not concern the reader, who will judge the product on its own merit.

Linz and Oxford   September 1988

Preface to the paperback edition

This book was completed in the autumn of 1988, and published in hardback almost a year later. Have the momentous events of the end of 1989 overtaken the argument presented here? In our view—they have not.

The objective of the book is to examine—theoretically and in the light of empirical evidence—the roots of the failure of the Marx-inspired economic system of socialism, and hence the reasons behind the search for market-oriented remedies. We try to trace the twists and bends of this difficult search which, if consistently pursued, cannot but lead to what we call 'market socialism proper' (MS). Despite the fact that MS is tantamout to renunciation of what has long been perceived as fundamentals of socialism as a distinct economic system, the term itself seems to us justified for a description of the last station on the tortuous, and ultimately futile, reformist road. 'Real socialism' has proved unreformable, and even MS would exhibit more disadvantages than advantages in comparison with a private market economy.

In the course of the anti-communist revolution in Eastern Europe public opinion turned against any form of socialism, MS included. However, an instant transition from a command to a market economy looks impossible, first of all because of property relations. Firms belonging to the state in one form or another will therefore remain important in the economy for quite a time, especially in industry, and hence some 'cohabitation' between a sizeable state sector and a growing private sector seems unavoidable. Such 'cohabitation' may be viewed as an MS forced upon society on its way towards private market economy. This is another reason why we believe the problems discussed in our book remain relevant for understanding the process of decomposition of communism.

W.B.
K.L.

Contents

PART I

Marxist Socialism—the Promise

I

The Claim to Economic Rationality

Our intention in this chapter is not to go over the whole ground of the Marxist theory of communist socio-economic formation, the first stage of which is defined as socialism. This ground is pretty well covered not only in numerous past writings, but in most recent ones as well.[1] What we want to do is to concentrate on those aspects of the theory which may be regarded as closest to contemporary economic dilemmas, in the light of the Marxist claim that socialism surpasses its predecessor—capitalism—in terms of economic rationality.

Economic rationality need not be a part of the 'case for socialism', or at least need not be the decisive part. Certain socialists expect economic problems actually to be solved, and conditions for the comprehensive satisfaction of material human needs to be established, prior to the emergence of socialism as such; some of them even maintain in this context that 'socialism's distinctive means of production is leisure.'[2] Then there is the non-Marxist tradition, particularly strong in British Fabianism, which rejects capitalism primarily on ethical grounds of social justice, although challenges of political practice since the 1930s had to be met also with wider elaboration of the economic case for advocating the advance towards socialism.[3] Another version of the emphasis on the broadly understood ethical side of socialism seems to emerge from the East European experience, which has led some writers to conclude that there might be a conflict between the ethical goals and the economic rationality of socialism, and hence a necessity to accept certain trade-offs.[4]

All these and similar points perhaps deserve careful consideration in another framework. However, in our understanding of Marxism the ethical superiority of socialism over capitalism is supposed to go hand-in-hand with economic superiority, the two reinforcing each other. Human emancipation under socialism, freeing the human being from oppression and injustice, becomes a condition and an indispensable factor in the liberation of productive forces from the fetters of obsolete capitalist relations of production. At the same time, the replacement of capitalist relations of production by socialist ones becomes a condition and an indispensable factor in human emancipation. The unity of the two aspects is rooted conceptually in the notion of *social* ownership of the means of production.

Social ownership of the means of production is a complex notion transcending the conceptual framework of property rights in the Roman legal tradition, although the language of the latter may perhaps be useful in distinguishing social ownership from ownership in a conventional sense. So, if we take such a basic element of property rights as the exclusion of non-owners from control over the object of ownership, social ownership would have to be characterized as eliminating such exclusion for members of the society. In other words, social ownership of the means of production is supposed to grant to every member of the society the right of equal access to the decisions regarding the way those means of production are applied and the way the fruits of that application are distributed. Thus the concept of social ownership extends beyond that of *public* ownership, if by the latter it is meant that a public body is designated as the legal owner: to make it social, such a public body must be under the effective control of the society. This introduces immediately a whole range of most difficult problems of the forms of and the criteria for effective social control; in the case of the state as the owner the problem becomes political.[5]

Social ownership of the means of production is supposed to provide the basis for restoration of the balance ('correspondence') between modern productive forces and the system of production relations (the economic system, for short). The former are said to have outgrown an economic system founded on the fragmentation of economic activity by separately owned units, relating to each other only through the competitive spontaneity of market processes. According to Marxist theory, socialization of the means of production transforms labour into 'directly social', that is serving the needs of the society in a straightforward manner, as opposed to the 'indirectly social' labour under capitalism, where private profit considerations are interposed between the application of labour and the satisfaction of social needs. This transformation not only puts an end to subjugation of one human being to another (wage labour for someone else, exploitation) but also opens the way to rational organization of the entire economic activity of the society. The latter may be regarded as human emancipation in a broad sense—a change from dependence on elemental, ill-understood forces governing the economic processes to conscious regulation of these processes, with even the very system of regulation *designed*, and not simply inherited as an outcome of spontaneous development. We have here a clear reflection of Marxism's anthropological optimism: the firm belief in the human capacity to organize the economy (and social life in general) rationally when appropriate conditions are created. Socialism is supposed to create such conditions—to employ the usual distinction—for substantive and methodological rationality of economic behaviour on a society-wide scale.

The integration of separate units of economic activity into a society-wide whole on the basis of social ownership of the means of production is seen by Marxists as playing a paramount role here. Oskar Lange has paid particular attention to this attribute of socialism, which supposedly allows the raising of the criteria of rational behaviour from the private to the societal scale—or, in other words, from the microlevel to the macrolevel.[6] The significance of this lies not merely in 'internalization of externalities', that is in the possibility of taking into account costs and benefits outside the purview of microunits, but also in elimination of inefficiencies on a macroscale caused by pursuit of objectives rational only from the microeconomic point of view. Hence there arises Lange's proposition of the hierarchical structure of objectives as typical for a socialist economy: lower-rank objectives become the means for attaining higher-level ones, and the criteria for rational behaviour of the subsystems (sectors, branches, enterprises) are subordinated to those of the system as a whole. Central planning—*ex ante* coordination of economic activity on a macroscale—becomes a natural corollary, a necessary component of the directly social character of labour, linked intricately to the fundamental change in the principle of human behaviour in the economic sphere: from that of competition or rivalry to that of cooperation between associates. In the light of what has been said before about the unity of economic and ethical aspects in the Marxist theory of socialism, it would not be right to maintain that *Homo oeconomicus* is being replaced by *Homo socialis*, but the expectation of the two coalescing into one is clearly there.

The above is a maximally compressed picture of the Marxist approach to the problem of socialism's economic rationality. It leaves out many intermediate links, and therefore presents the theory impoverished—but seems to bring out its intrinsic logic. Among other things, this abstract logic, stripped of particularisms, shows perhaps more clearly than otherwise the incompatibility of the market with the scheme of a rational socialist economy according to Marx-ism. The market is an indispensable coordinating mechanism in a setting where the participants in the divison of labour are separated economically. Now, even without touching on the question of the division of labour (the utopian dreams of its disappearance may be relegated to the unforeseeably distant future), the element of separa-tion cannot be admitted into the—let us call it orthodox—Marxist scheme, except for purely organizational reasons, and then subject to a very strict implementation of the hierarchical structure of sub-ordination. Not only does private enterprise run counter to the logic of rational socialism in the above sense, but so also does collective enterprise through group ownership; Engels was therefore perfectly consistent when he attacked Dühring's communes,[7] and the attempts of the ideologues of Yugoslav self-management socialism to interpret some of Marx's writings in their favour appears rather misplaced.[8] This is not to say that one could not find in Marx passages compatible with a more benign attitude towards the market under socialism, but as far as the essence of the theory goes the conclusion looks indisputable.

By raising the criteria of rational behaviour from the microecon-omic to the macroeconomic level (without, however, spelling out the boundaries of the macroarea: national? international?), socialism is supposed to show major gains in efficiency compared with capitalism. Moreover, in the Marxist vision there is actually no room for trade-offs between lesser efficiency in one aspect against higher in another; gains are expected across the board—in the fuller utilization of available resources on a macroscale, in the more apposite allocation of resources between alternative ends and means, in higher X-efficiency.

The prospect of *full employment* of human and material resources constitutes the backbone of socialism's claim to economic superiority over capitalism. On no other issue has the criticism of capitalism's failure to create conditions for rational economic behaviour been so harsh and unequivocal. The gist of the conflict between the develop-ment potential of productive forces and the capitalist mode of production can be found in Marx's analysis of the absurdity of 'excess capital and excess population', brought about not by the saturation of needs but by the inadequacy of the aggregate effective demand generated periodically by the profit-oriented system:

Over-production of capital is never anything more than over-production of means of production which may serve as capital. . . . It is no contradiction that this over-production of capital is accompanied by more or less consider-able relative over-population. . . . If capital is sent abroad, this is not done because it absolutely could not be applied at home, but because it can be employed at a higher rate of profit in a foreign country. . . . There are not too many necessities of life produced, in proportion to the existing popu-lation. Quite the reverse. Too little is produced decently and humanly to satisfy the wants of the great mass. There are not too many means of production to employ the able-bodied population. Quite the reverse. . . . Not enough means of production are produced to permit the employment of the entire able-bodied population under the most productive conditions, so that their absolute working period could be shortened by the mass and effective-ness of the constant capital employed during working hours. On the other hand, too many means of labour and necessities of life are produced at times to permit their serving as a means of exploitation of labourers at a certain rate of profit. Too many commodities are produced to permit of a realization and conversion into new capital of the value and surplus-value contained in them under the conditons of distribution and consumption peculiar to capitalist production, i.e. too many to permit the consummation of this process without constantly recurring explosions. Not too much wealth is produced. But at times too much wealth is produced in its capitalistic, self-contradictory form.[9]

The promise of socialism to do away with this form of waste became especially topical under the impact of the Great Depression of the 1930s, and it was this aspect of the economic case for socialism which clearly dominated not only Marxist thinking, but also that of other socialists—including the British neo-Fabians—before and in the aftermath of World War II. It was strongly felt that whatever the merits of fine tuning of the transformation and substitution ratios (in textbook terms of the allocative efficiency of the market mechanism), or the organizational gains within the microunit, or even the increase in the amount of resources available (including those due to techno-logical innovation and education), their macroeconomic and social effects depend on the degree of utilization of resources, limited under capitalism by the inadequacy of and fluctuations in aggregate demand.

Several factors are expected to make socialism capable of overcom-ing the unseemly coexistence of excess capital, unemployed labour, and unsatisfied needs. First, socialism should generate the natural tendency, uninhibited by private profit considerations, to use to the full the existing potential for economic development. Needs in the broad sense, that is including qualitative aspects, can never be regarded as satiated; hence there should be a strong propensity to invest, prompted by the desire to satisfy needs. Secondly, for evident reasons, a socialist government should be expected to be committed to full employment of labour, and hence to strive for an appropriate balance between capital intensity and labour intensity in its invest-ment policy (including replacement of obsolete equipment). Thirdly—and this is perhaps the most general point—socialism should be capable of harmonizing the distribution of national product with the output potential on a macroscale through flexible adjustment of prices and wages. As Kalecki maintains, 'whatever the rate of growth, the productive resources [under socialism] are fully utilized because of . . . price flexibility: prices are pushed . . . in relation to wages up to the point where the real income of labour and thus its consumption is adequate to cause the absorption of full employment national product.'[10] It ought to be clear that what is meant here is not the flexibility of relative prices of particular goods and services under the impact of the changing supply and demand position in the market-place, but the flexibility of the macroproportion between profits (investment) and wages (consumption). In other words, whereas under capitalism output (and hence employment) is being adjusted to a given distribution (relationship between profits and wages), socialism is said to be capable of adjusting distribution (changing relationship between profits and wages) to full employment output. This means that full employment under socialism is not entirely and constantly dependent on expansionary policies with high investment activity: if the latter fell for any reason, wages would rise in relation to prices, consumer demand would take over the appropri-ate part of investment demand, and savings at full employment level would again match investment *ex ante*, albeit at a lower level. Needless to say, neither of the afore-mentioned factors can in itself eliminate immediately the 'classical' unemployment due to physical shortage of capital, but consistent macropolicy of accumulation would be ex-pected to overcome this bottleneck in due course.

The notion of *allocative efficiency* does not appear explicitly in Marxist political economy, but the superiority of socialism in the allocation of resources between alternative ends and means is obviously implied. The claim in this respect rests, first, on the proposition that under socialism resources can be allocated without the waste involved in an *ex post* adjustment of the structure of supply to the structure of demand through spontaneous market regulation. It is in this context that the advantages of extending intrafactory planning—with well-defined goals and careful deployment of means—to the macroecon-omic sphere appealed so strongly to Marx and his followers: central planning was to secure steady movement of the economy along an equilibrium path, identified *ex ante* at both the output and the input ends, allowing each link in the social division of labour to fall directly into its proper place. The claim of central planning to be capable of charting in advance the course of economic development and to coordinate the activities in particular sectors along this course impressed many non-Marxists as well. This was one of the main reasons that led Schumpeter, for instance, to proclaim the superiority of the 'socialist blueprint':

There are cases in which capitalist industries are so circumstanced that prices and output become theoretically indeterminate. ... In a socialist economy everything—limiting cases without practical importance alone excepted—is uniquely determined. But even when there exists a theoretically determined state it is much more difficult and expensive to reach in the capitalist economy than it would be in the socialist economy. In the former endless moves and countermoves are necessary and decisions have to be taken in an atmosphere of uncertainty that blunts the edge of action, whereas that strategy and that uncertainty will be absent from the latter. ... This means more than it seems at first sight. Those determinate solutions of the problem of production are rational or optimal from the standpoint of given data, and anything that shortens, smoothens or safeguards the road that leads to them is bound to save human energy and material resources, and to reduce the costs at which a given result is attained. Unless the resources thus saved are completely wasted, efficiency in our sense must necessarily increase.[11]

Socialism's claim to allocative efficiency extends, however, beyond the advantages of 'unique determinateness' through macroeconomic planning, which can after all be regarded as a formal procedure indifferent to the contents of the *ex ante* coordination. Hence there arises the second prop on which the claim rests: the possibility of adequately defining the objectives of the production process. Production ceases to be dictated by competing entrepreneurs employing powerful methods of persuasion to induce the public to buy regardless of the usefulness of their wares, or by 'sovereign' consumers whose aggregate structure of demand is determined by distribution of income and wealth related neither to social justice nor to the economic contribution of the holders. Production under socialism is to be geared to the satisfaction of needs, which in turn can be ascertained directly by the planners representing the interests of the community, undistorted by class conflicts and inequitable distribution of purchasing power. In the same vein, the planners are to be capable of assessing the true outlays of direct and indirect (means of production) labour costs associated with a particular amount and composition of output. Together, planned regulation of social division of labour, corresponding to needs related to just distributional structure and assessed for social costs, is supposed to generate an allocation pattern which ought to satisfy the criteria of Pareto optimality. Taking into account what has been said above about the setting of objectives, these criteria should be met not in a formal but in a meaningful way, thus resulting in the clear allocational superiority of socialism over capitalism.

The concept of *X-efficiency* is relatively new in economic theory. It was introduced by Leibenstein in 1966 to correct the standard assumption that competitive market pressure automatically takes care of the best possible use of resources within each economic unit (cost minimization):

What I have called 'X-efficiency theory' is concerned with the type of inefficiency resulting from missed opportunities to utilize existing resources within productive organizations. . . . It is concerned with all types of non-allocative inefficiency. . . . Basically, what is involved are all types of inefficiencies resulting from the complete or partial lack of motivation to use economic opportunities as effectively as they might be used.[12]

If the existence of X-inefficiencies under capitalism is accepted (Marxist criticism of capitalism seems to have been as equally oblivious to them as has been neoclassicial microeconomics), social-ism gains another point because a socialist productive organization is supposed to be X-efficient. However, this is for reasons diametrically different from those assumed by the standard minimization postulate: it is not market pressure but integration of individual and group interests with those of the community as a whole which ought to bring the appropriate motivation. Liberation from an oppressive social order is expected to lead to overcoming of 'alienation' of individuals from the society, and hence to manifestly positive and creative attitudes to work and other duties. This, as observed earlier, is not to say that attitudes of *Homo oeconomicus* are simply replaced by altruism: self-interest does not disappear as a motive, but is perceived as going hand-in-hand with the communal one. In conjunction with socialist ownership of the means of production, this should result in the fading away of the distinction between the posture of a principal and that of an agent: instead a singular kind of behaviour, let us call it 'quasi-principal', with all the proper concerns for common good and responsibility for risks, ought to become the rule.

The motivation to utilize fully existing resources within productive organizations extends obviously to innovations, with regard both to products and to technology. Under socialism it is again not market pressure but the integration of self-interest with the common interest which is supposed to make economic actors eager to innovate. The motivation factor is amplified by the removal of macroeconomic obstacles to innovation:

1 No reason for any type of 'luddism', that is resistance to technical progress on the part of the workers under threat of becoming redundant; on the contrary, workers should expect only to gain, as both consumers and producers (shorter working time).
2 No reasons for resistance from the managers either; they ought not to fear the loss in value of the existing capital, which would be subject to national policy of scrapping and redeployment.
3 Central planners—facing supply-side constraints in their tendency to foster development—should obviously be interested in increased factor productivity, and hence in stimulating innovation, promoting appropriate education, and securing adequate funding of R&D.
4 Abolition of commercial secrecy should facilitate the spread of technical and organizational information, the exchange of experience, and so on—all factors of substantial significance for the generation, practical absorption, and dissemination of innovations.

At this point it is necessary to mention the well-known qualification of the motivation factor under conditions of socialism as the first stage of communist socio-economic formation. This is that the new, X-efficiency securing, attitudes are not assumed as prevailing straight away with the establishment of the new order. The claim made is that of a process unfolding under the educational impact of socialist reality. Along with full employment and elimination of cyclical fluctuations, distributional justice is taken as of paramount importance for this process. First, income from capital ('unearned income') is eliminated as a result of socialization of ownership of the means of production; secondly, there is a more equitable size distribution of incomes; and thirdly, the social services and benefits provided out of communal means—among other things to help equalize opportunities—are expected to grow *pari passu* with or rather faster than the growth of output of the society as a whole.

The recognition that 'dis-alienation' and its effects for motivation cannot be taken for granted from the very outset has led to an acknowledgement of the need to use initially direct material stimulation of individuals and groups. Economic incentives in this context are supposed to fulfil a double task: to substitute for the original inadequacy of 'social mindedness' (this is the bourgeois principle of *do ut des*, proclaimed by Marx in the *Critique of the Gotha Programme* as the 'according to work' criterion of distribution during the 'lower stage of communism'); and to become another educational device by showing in practice that enhancement of social well-being enhances one's own as well. However, resorting to economic incentives—otherwise a welcome sign of realism—introduces into the postulated system an alien element threatening to come into conflict with the basic assumptions of the model. The problem immediately arising is that of the valuation and commensurability of contribution and remuneration, in both absolute and relative terms. This category of problem has been either totally neglected by Marxist theoreticians before the Russian Revolution, or at best taken very lightly as solvable with increasing ease thanks to the nature of the development process itself, which simplifies the task of direct economic calculation (smaller number of bigger choices) on the one hand, and improves continuously the computational tools on the other. Largely similar has been the attitude towards the danger of conflicting interests being generated by an incentive principle of distribution, and the possibility of their consequences spreading also to the informational sphere (report distortions, bargaining); again the development process, in this case of the 'proletarian consciousness', ought to create the conditions for reducing the danger to manageable dimensions.

There is no point in examining at this stage the validity of this fundamentalist Marxist claim to socialism's economic rationality, and in particular in trying to set apart the obviously utopian elements from those of more pragmatic relevance; conclusions of this sort should emerge later from our discussion of the economics of 'real socialism'. However, what is necessary is to emphasize that the claim presented above has been clearly predicated upon socialism succeeding mature capitalism, which has outgrown its usefulness as an engine of progress in accordance with Marx's assertion that 'no social order ever perishes before all the productive forces for which there is room in it have developed; and new higher relations of production never appear before the material conditions of their existence have matured in the womb of the old society itself.'[13] The link between the overripeness of capitalism and the rationale for socialism has evidently been accepted by Schumpeter too, although he certainly cannot be associated with Marxist optimism in respect of socialism's dynamic prospects, or with the marketless version of the future economic order. Among the most important 'observable tendencies' in the Schumpeterian 'march into socialism' is supposedly the waning role of the entrepreneurial function, which constitutes the cornerstone of Schumpeter's own theory of economic development. Other 'crumbling walls' of capitalism are closely interconnected, as the following quotation distinctly illustrates:

Most of the argument of Part II ['Can Capitalism Survive?'] may be summed up in the Marxian proposition that the economic process tends to socialize *itself*—and also the human soul. By this we mean that the technological, organizational, commercial, administrative and psychological prerequisites of socialism tend to be fulfilled more and more. Let us . . . visualize the state of things which looms in the future if that trend be projected. Business, excepting the agrarian sector, is controlled by a small number of bureaucratized corporations. Progress has slackened and become mechanized and planned. The rate of interest converges toward zero, not temporarily only or under pressure of governmental policy, but permanently owing to the dwindling of investment opportunities. Industrial property and management have become depersonalized—ownership having degenerated to stock and bond holding, the executives having acquired habits of mind similar to those of civil servants. Capitalist motivation and standards have all but wilted away. The inference as to the transition to a socialist regime in such fullness of time is obvious.[14]

The previous paragraph shows clearly the relationship between Schumpeter and Marx in the matter: in Schumpeter's perception the advent of socialism is not a cause for celebration, even though he acknowledges some possible positive features of a socialist economy, as for instance its expected capacity to overcome fluctuations. However, the difference in valuation notwithstanding, he shares with Marx the belief that history is on socialism's side, and hence that socialism is the legitimate successor to capitalism, the very development of which creates prerequisites for socialism's economic rationality.

In view of the affirmation of the 'march into socialism' by such otherwise divergent thinkers, the question deserves more detailed examination. This may help to assess both the foundations of the Marxist theory of socialism itself, and the degree to which the experience of 'real socialism' can be taken as a testing ground for the validity of the claim to socialism's economic superiority.

PART II

Real Socialism—the Disappointments

The term 'real socialism' or 'really existing socialism' was contrived in the Brezhnev era as an arrogant antithesis to the reformist ideas of 'genuine' socialism, and particularly to the 'socialism with a human face' of the 1968 Prague Spring. No other socialism exists and can exist apart from the one created under the leadership of the communist parties in power: that has been the intended message of the term. Whatever the intentions, the term proved useful as a designation of the political and socio-economic order existing in the countries ruled by communist parties, regardless of the differences between their levels of development, their domestic policies and institutions, and their international course. It covered conveniently the Soviet Union and her East European allies belonging both to the Warsaw Pact and the Council of Mutual Economic Assistance (CMEA or Comecon), the non-European Comecon members (Mongolia, Cuba, Vietnam), and the 'other socialist countries' (Yugoslavia, Albania, China, Laos and Kampuchea), and it could easily incorporate those classified in the 1986 Soviet party programme as 'countries of socialist orientation' (a number of African countries, and presumably Nicaragua) when the politically appropriate moment came.

We shall use the term 'real socialism' accordingly, as a value-free designation of the area under communist rule. Such a single mark is especially opportune for our analysis, which concentrates on common features of the evolution of the system, and not on national peculiarities. A proviso must be added, however: the basis of our generalizations about 'real socialism' is confined to the experience of the Soviet Union, East European communist countries, and to some extent China.

The Historical Regularity in Reverse

'Real socialism' was proudly proclaimed by its leaders, and widely regarded by most people, to be a child of Marxism. However, it was an embarassing child because it seems to contradict the Marxist 'laws of motion' of the historical process, which was supposed to deliver socialism out of the womb of a mature capitalist system. The twentieth century played havoc with this assertion.

For the orthodox followers of Marxist historical materialism, with its strong deterministic component, the challenge came with the 1917 revolution in Russia. Faithful to the doctrine, most non-Bolshevik Marxists, including such luminaries as Karl Kautsky, denied the socialist character of the revolution in a predominantly peasant country with mere islands of industrial development and scant cultural and organizational conditions for planned management of the economy. Since then quite a number of Marxists have consistently refused to accept the socialist credentials of the Soviet Union and other countries which followed in her footsteps. They also deny the validity of checking the claim to socialism's economic rationality and human emancipation against communist experience. In their view, both socialism and Marxism remain unscathed by this bastard product of the rape of history.

On the other hand, there have been plenty of attempts to reconcile the main body of the theory with this deflection from the predicted line of the dialectical interaction between the development of productive forces and production relations. In the aftermath of World War I, and perhaps during the interwar period as a whole, the arguments of this strand might look as not entirely deprived of plausibility. The less committed argued simply that the incongruity of the victory of the revolution in Russia, as against the defeat in Germany and the lack of revolutionary situations in other major industrialized countries, could be regarded as a historical accident, a temporary freak unsuitable for generalizations. The dominant line, adopted by the communist wing of Marxism and made part and parcel of the official ideology in all countries of 'real socialism', was far more assertive, trying to justify the actual developments in a positive way. Based on Lenin's (and in fact to some extent also on Trotsky's) formula of 'uneven development of capitalism in its imperialist stage', the postulate of maturity was reinterpreted as applying to the capitalist system as a whole, on the world scale. With world capitalism being sufficiently advanced for socialist transformation, the revolutionary break of the chain in the politically weakest link becomes legitimate. The Great Depression of the 1930s, by throwing the capitalist economy into an unprecedented downswing, bringing disastrous misery to many millions around the world, and acute instability in political relations, seemed to add weight to the argument: capitalism survived, owing to the political skills and brutal physical force mobilized by the bourgeoisie, contrary to the laws of socio-economic development; this makes its survival increasingly costly, and ultimately only temporary. There can be little doubt that it was the turbulence in the capitalist economy at the time and the growing perception of the need to resort to regulatory and redistributionary state economic policies to combat the crisis that also made many non-Marxists more receptive to the idea of the 'march into socialism'; one can detect such a connection in Schumpeter as well. A related factor was the apparent contrast between the capitalist world and the picture of rapid growth and elimination of the plague of unemployment presented by the Soviet economy—without disclosing the dark side of the socialist moon.

It is not our intention to probe now into the validity of these arguments, and particularly into the question of the true Soviet performance of the time. The only point we want to make here is that despite the setbacks to the socialist revolution in industrial countries, the realities of the interwar period still left room for interpretations compatible with the Marxist concept of the historical regularity of the movement toward socialism.

In the aftermath of World War II this interpretation could still be argued for, but with its plausibility diminishing over time. On the credit side was placed first the Soviet war success, presented as an unequivocal test of the socialist system's viability and strength; then the very fact of further expansion of socialism to new countries and continents; and finally the widespread view that problems of postwar reconstruction and restructuralization in the industrial world required socialist methods of economic management in order to prevent repetition of the interwar debacle. On the other hand, however, the Marxist version of the 'laws of motion' towards socialism

suffered severe setbacks: the expansion into Eastern Europe was evidently imposed by force, and wherever a claim to the endogeneity of the transition to socialism could be made with any justification, this was at best, as in Yugoslavia, in countries at a level of development comparable with that of pre-revolutionary Russia. In all other cases—China, and later Cuba or Vietnam—communist parties came to power in conditions of very much deeper economic retardation. Combined with the survival of the capitalist order in the leading industrial countries, this could not so easily be explained again either as a freak or as a manifestation of the 'uneven development of capitalism in its imperialist stage'. The suspicion of something like reverse regularity—the lower the level of economic and social development, the better the chances for a socialist revolution— was inevitably looming larger. Not the classical Marxist conflicts between the proletariat and bourgeoisie, but the struggle against colonial exploitation and national subjugation, were the driving forces of such a revolution; and not the fuller utilization of the economic potential created by capitalism, but the promise of deliverance from underdevelopment, destitution, and ignorance, made socialism attractive. This was acknowledged by Joan Robinson, who—sympathetic to socialism, but free of Marxist insistence on the laws of history—tried to generalize the empirical evidence in a new formula of socialism, not 'as a stage beyond capitalism but a substitute for it—a means by which the nations which did not share in the Industrial Revolution can imitate its technical achievements, a means of achieving rapid accumulation under a different set of rules of the game'.[1]

The notion of socialism not as a successor to but as a substitute for capitalism in less developed countries was, obviously, unacceptable to Marxists, and numerous attempts were made to refute it. Among others, one of the present authors argued that although it was true that imitation of the capitalist road of development—apart from very exceptional circumstances—would be impossible for the less developed countries in the second half of the twentieth century, the rationale of the socialist way was asserting itself not because of their immaturity but in spite of it.[2] It was hardly a convincing argument, partly because of the mixed evidence on the comparative success of the capitalist and socialist strategies of fighting backwardness, but mainly because it missed the point about the historical regularities which—regardless of the results achieved under a socialist system in the less developed parts of the world—must be tested in the leading countries. And it was precisely in this testing ground that developments in the second half of the twentieth century began to undermine forcefully the concept of the 'march into socialism', both in the Marxist and in the Schumpeterian version.

Unlike in the interwar period, surviving capitalism since World War II has avoided plunging into depression. Indeed, fluctuations notwithstanding—and those were rather mild by the standards of the 1930s—the Western economies displayed, for at least a quarter of a century from the end of the postwar recovery, a truly remarkable dynamic capacity: high rates of growth of output and popular consumption; low (in many cases practically nil) unemployment; a strong propensity to innovate both in methods of production and in final products; and a substantial widening of social provision (the 'welfare state'). Even discounting cases of exceptional dynamism (for instance Japan), the capitalist West looked in this period to be anything but a system of production relations putting fetters on productive forces. There were obviously differences in performance between individual countries, but not of the kind which would allow easy categorization in systemic terms or in terms of relative levels of development; Italy, Greece, and Spain surged ahead along with France, Germany, and Scandinavia, and several Asian market economies (South Korea, Taiwan, Hong Kong, Singapore) managed a dramatic jump from underdevelopment to the hastily established category of 'newly industrialized countries' (NICs). Moreover, the process of rapid technological change, the emergence of new centres of modern industry, the greater interdependence of individual economies owing to a powerful expansion in the international movement of goods, capital, and labour—all this caused a wide-ranging transformation of the population structure in the developed capitalist West, weakening the familiar social factors relied upon by the Marxist expectations of the 'march into socialism'. The fall of the relative and then absolute numbers of manual workers in general, and those employed in the traditional proletarian strongholds of the 'smokestack' industries in particular, coupled with a marked increase in prosperity and the ownership of consumer wealth (houses, durables), not only reduced the scale of support for political militancy but also gave a strong push to the advance of what may be described as 'middle-class attitudes'—a tendency to seek improvement within and not outside the existing socio-economic system.

For a time capitalism's new dynamism was ignored by Marxist literature, especially in communist countries, but elsewhere as well.

When the problem could no longer be ignored and was faced, mainly by the protagonists of 'open Marxism', the attempted defence of the historical trend toward socialist transformation went in the direction of explaining the reasons for success by the socialist nature of the policies applied: the rise of state interventionism, bordering in some cases on macroeconomic indicative planning; substantial growth of the public sector in production; an even greater increase in the share of public spending in total expenditures; and a host of other forms of regulatory and redistributional measures undertaken by the 'visible hand'. In other words, capitalism was being saved by the gradual introduction of socialism, in what was to be read as a sign of the historical tendency reasserting itself. Moreover, it was alleged that the resolution of conflicts which continued to be generated by the still dominant private capital would require further extension of the socialist components in the economic system. In this way the validity of the 'march into socialism' was kept alive.

It is beyond the scope of this work to undertake an analysis of factors determining or influencing postwar Western performance. There is no doubt that on the whole a correlation could be found between the major period of economic progress and the increase in the role of the state. However, such a correlation must not necessarily be interpreted as evidence in favour of the 'march into socialism'. Even at the peak of state interventionism the Western economies remained basically regulated by the market. The state interfered with the operation of the market, but at no stage did there appear the prospect of replacing the market by direct allocation of resources of the kind envisaged in the Marxist blueprint. In particular the opportunity for entrepreneurship was preserved, and contrary to Schumpeter's expectations the entrepreneurial function flourished, resulting in the explosive spread of new technologies and new products in commercial use throughout the world.

Around the mid 1970s the long Western boom came to an end; the familiar problems of excess capacity and unemployment returned to the economic agenda. However, the response to these problems was different from what might have been expected by traditional Marxists—politically, in the actual evolution of the economic system, and intellectually. Politically, probably as at least a partial reflection of the social changes mentioned earlier, the non-socialist parties were on the whole gaining at the expense of the Left. In the economy, a shift occurred towards deregulation and privatization, while the attempts to widen the public sector and to increase state intervention-ism (France, Greece) were rather quickly put into reverse. Intellec-tually, not only was there manifest a rise in *laissez-faire* ideology among those leaning politically to the Right or to the Centre, but even on the Left the radical socialist solutions were losing support relative to the moderate stand. Characteristic in this respect was the strong revival of the idea of 'market socialism' in the British Labour Party, not as a temporary pragmatic compromise but as a fundamen-tal systemic feature.[3] Needless to say, the deteriorating economic performance of the countries of 'real socialism' and their increasingly frequent recourse to marketization as a cure must have contributed to this kind of response to the reappearance of the capitalist contra-dictions in the developed West.

Although we raise the issues of the 1980s, we do not intend in any sense to become involved in the dispute about the relative roles of the 'visible' and 'invisible' hands in dealing with the complex national and international economic problems of the Western world. We refer to them only from the perspective of the Marxist proposition of the existence of an objective tendency toward socialism. Such tendency cannot be, in our opinion, discerned in the mature capitalist societies when they approach the end of the century. By this we mean not that there is a lack of forces acting in the socialist direction, but instead that with the passage of time these forces become weaker rather than stronger.

For the Marxist vision of the rational socialist economy, this conclusion seems to have a twofold significance. First, it reveals the fallacy of, or at least the lack of supporting evidence for, one of the fundamental tenets of the Marxist model of a socialist/communist economy, which is supposed to be a product of the historical regularity of development. Secondly, in a paradoxical way it legitim-izes the confrontation of the model with the realities of 'real socialism' as a procedure for verifying the claim to socialism's economic rationality, if not in its whole then at least in substantial part. Whether we accept the existence of a reverse regularity or the absence of any regularity at all in the transition to socialism, the cases available for examination have to be treated as normal, including the problems they present with regard to the separation of the general from the particular.

3

The Objective of Catching Up

Whether by caprice or by the perverse regularity of history, one of the main common features of the countries of 'real socialism' is that they started their transition to socialism under conditions of immaturity in orthodox Marxist (and Schumpeterian) terms. Hence the overriding objective of the victorious revolution was to eliminate the retardation, economically as well as socially and culturally. Of course, such an objective could not in the first instance be formulated even by the greatest optimists in a country unable to meet certain preconditions: size, endowment of natural resources, and the existence of some initial industrial base. Russia satisfied these conditions, and thus became the blazer of a hitherto untried and unexpected trail. Lenin made the point unambiguously, coming out in one of his last articles once more against the traditional view that Russia had not reached the level of development of productive forces necessary for the construction of socialism:

If for the creation of socialism a definite level of culture is required (although nobody can say what precisely is this definite 'level of culture'), why is it not permissible to begin at the start from acquiring in a revolutionary way the premises of this definite level, and then *later*, on the foundation of the workers' and peasants' power and the Soviet order, to get to the task of overtaking other nations? ... I recall that Napoleon has written: 'On s'engage et puis ... on voit.' In a free translation this means: 'First we have to engage ourselves in a serious battle, and then we shall see.'[1]

These words reflect precisely the essence of the Bolshevik idea of building socialism under conditions of immaturity: to use the power of the state to drag the economy out of backwardness and reach the level 'required for socialism'. In another of Lenin's pronouncements, with electrification as the symbol of modernization in general, the matter found its most concise and famous formula: 'Communism = Soviet power + electrification of the entire country.' The use of state power in accomplishing the task of economic modernization and 'overtaking of other nations' should be understood not only as the takeover of most of the nation's physical capital (means of production), but also as state control over the entire process of allocation and implementation of resources, with special emphasis on securing the level of accumulation and structure of investment deemed necessary. This obviously has wide political implications as well.

The policy of economic modernization of communist countries was made operative through the system of national planning. In practice the long-term plans (for 15 or 20 years), although worked out from time to time almost everywhere, proved less important than the medium-term ones, mainly the five-year plans which in the interwar period acquired such fame (Soviet *pyatiletkas*). These medium-term plans obviously differed in specific tasks and quantitative relationships between individual countries and periods, but when looked at in their sequence and from the point of view of the construction of socialism they display basic similarities in what may be understood broadly as the underlying development strategy. Because of its link with the process of transition to socialism under conditions of immaturity, and because of the fact that it was pursued in all countries of 'real socialism' in some phase of their development, this strategy may be called socialist or communist modernization strategy. It should be remembered however that it emerged first in the USSR in the 1920s, and consequently must have reflected not only general ideas of modernization on the way to socialism, but also the peculiar Soviet conditions of the time. These included a vast territory, mostly underpopulated, and rich in not easily accessible natural resources; on the whole an unfavourable climate and below average soil conditions for agriculture; a hostile external environment (whatever the true origins of this hostility), which pushed politico-military objectives to the top of the list of priorities; and a lack of experience in designing a macrostrategy, compounded by ideological rigidities and the political suppression of those in search of alternatives. These peculiarities have not been sufficiently acknowledged in the official communist ideology, which elevated the Soviet development strategy to that of a universal model. As such it was after World War II either imposed on (Eastern Europe) or adopted by (China) other countries of 'real socialism' with only minor modifications, although at some point it might have looked as if the Chinese were set on more significant changes. Yugoslavia, initially also imitating the Soviet strategy, moved away after the 1948 break, but more in respect of the institutional framework for the development process than in terms of macroeconomic policies.

The Soviet or Soviet-type strategy of economic modernization has a vast analytical literature[2] which makes superflous any attempt to describe it in detail here. We shall therefore limit ourselves to the following three-point summary of the strategy.

The first factor was the very fast growth of industry ('rapid industrialization drive') through massive investment in new industrial capacity. This required a sharp and abrupt rise in the share of accumulation in national income (the rate of accumulation) at the expense of the share of consumption. Theoretically the fall in consumption need not be absolute; it could be relative to the levels that would have obtained without acceleration. In practice, however, an absolute decline in the initial period was the rule, particularly with regard to real remuneration per employee as distinct from consumption per head. Although the losses in consumption were not planned, either in the Soviet first five-year plan or in the corresponding plans of the East European countries, they should be regarded *a posteriori* as a part of the strategy, while the optimistic scenarios of a parallel increase in both investment and consumption should be seen as mainly wishful thinking. Two important assumptions were implicit in the acceptance of sacrifices in consumption. One was that the sacrifices were only temporary, because in the long run consumption would certainly be higher than it otherwise would have been without acceleration. In terms of growth theory,[3] such certainty could be justified only under non-increasing technical coefficients (particularly incremental capital/output ratios or ICORs), and stable growth, which proved unrealistic. The other assumption was that any fall in real earnings per employee would be compensated by rising family incomes because of an increase in employment, which was to be the main primary resource for the initial industrialization drive. Again, such compensation often proved not to occur, and even when it did the income implications were haphazard and without connection to the work performed. With regard to the distribution of the accumulation burden between social classes, the original idea was to shift it mainly to the peasantry. This failed, either because of the necessity (as in the USSR) to avoid complete collapse of agriculture in the wake of the collectivization disaster by directing additional investment to the countryside, or because the idea was abandoned more (China) or less (Eastern Europe) explicitly. This is to say not that the peasantry did not suffer enormously (although probably nowhere else to the same extent as in the USSR), but merely that the sufferings extended to the population as a whole, industrial workers included.

The second principle in the Soviet strategy was selective, unbalanced growth, with resources directed to sectors and activities designated as the 'engines of growth'. In this way a short-cut was to be accomplished, without waiting for inducements coming from the demand side through the usual sequence of consumption, agriculture, light industry, and heavy industry. In fact this order was categorically reversed by Stalin:[4] there was to be priority of investment over consumption, of industry over agriculture, of heavy industry (especially engineering) over light industry, of production over infrastructure, and of education (particularly technical and vocational) over housing. Selectivity applied also to techniques of production. Modern technology was limited not simply to high-priority sectors, but even to high-priority operations coexisting with very primitive methods elsewhere (for instance, in intraplant transport). Among other things, forced labour and to a lesser extent mobilization campaigns could be regarded as methods of capital saving (needless to say, this was not the only aspect of the economic significance of forced labour in the industrialization drive). Anyhow, the principle expressed in the famous Chinese catch-phrase 'walking on two legs' was put into practice in the Soviet Union and Eastern Europe as well, although not so drastically as in Chinese backyard metal production.

The third strategic factor was the maximal utilization of the existing resources of capital and labour in defiance of conventional cost calculations, particularly at the microlevel. This took a variety of forms. The most important was probably the extension of output and employment beyond the point justified by profitability criteria; this was done *inter alia* by raising the number of shifts and taking on less skilled labour. A fast increase in output was essential, particularly in the first stage of the huge investment programme when new capacities were being created but had not yet begun to operate. At the same time, however, the tendency to maximize current output and employment went against the requirement of maximizing the reinvestable surplus.[5] This was a clear conflict of objectives, again resolved usually by an additional squeeze on wages, not in money terms but through open, hidden, or suppressed inflation; the neglect of housing, in the fields both of construction and of maintenance and repairs, belonged to the same category. The preservation of physically usable but economically obsolescent equipment was another expression of disregarding costs in favour of output. A theoretical justification was found for this approach in the claim that socialism abolishes the 'moral obsolescence' of capital equipment. One also might assign to this feature of Soviet-type development strategy the predominance of import substitution (as distinct from comparative advantage) in foreign trade policy. The rejection of the principle of comparative advantage could be seen also in the attempt to create in every single country, regardless of its size and natural endowment, a comprehensive industrial structure as self-sufficient as possible, particularly in metals. The enormous and ubiquitous steel complexes throughout Eastern Europe became a sort of symbol of this policy, which to some extent must have been dictated by military consideration in accordance with the then prevailing doctrine.

This most concise summary fits best the policies actually pursued up to the mid 1950s, or the late 1950s as far as China is concerned. The changes that occurred subsequently were numerous and multi-directional, but did not amount to a coherent new strategy. Some of them will be discussed later in connection with systemic reforms, but from the point of view of the problems examined here we can limit ourselves to what has been said above.

How successful was the Soviet-type strategy in overcoming the immaturity obstacles to the creation of a socialist society? Although this seems the right question to ask in the context of the theory of the 'march into socialism', its legitimacy becomes doubtful in the light of the experience of 'real socialism'. Achieving maturity in economic, social, and cultural structures was regarded as necessary—by both Marx and Schumpeter—in order to make the transition to socialism natural, corresponding to the requirements of further development. In other words, modernization comes first, and then generates the process of transformation of the social order. What actually happened in the countries of 'real socialism' was the reverse: the transformation of the social order—nationalization of the means of production, central planning as the main regulating device instead of the market, and so on—occurred either before or at best in the early stages of the modernization drive, and came to be regarded as its indispensable counterpart. Of course, the objective of establishing the new social order was never reduced to its modernizing function. The socialist transformation of society, as defined by the Communist Party, was an objective in itself, the doctrinal interpretation of which often clashed with purely developmental interests; the struggle against the frequently demonized if not outright invented class enemy inflicted heavy losses on the economies of 'real socialism', and the daunting Soviet experience, particularly with the collectivization of agriculture accompanied by the 'elimination of the kulaks as a class', did little to ward off similar type of damage in other countries. Nevertheless, the task of modernization was always there, and even the doctrinal excesses were justified by the Communist Party leadership as necessary to create favourable systemic conditions for unfettered economic development.

Thus the practice of 'real socialism', rather in accordance with Lenin's position presented earlier, meant not only a reversal of the time sequence in relation to the expected course of events (modernization after, instead of before, the revolution), but a basic shift in the perceived line of dependence: socialism was to be not the outcome but the major vehicle of 'overtaking other nations'. Hence the right question to ask about the effects of Soviet-type development strategy is how well it served the objective of catching up, bearing in mind that it was inextricably linked with specific form of socialist transformation of the economy, as well as of the polity and of the entire fabric of social relations.

Needless to say, any attempt to answer this question involves enormous complexities, as can be seen in the huge economic literature on the long-term performance of the USSR, Eastern Europe, and China, especially in a comprehensive comparative perspective.[6] Moreover the problem lies not only, and perhaps not mainly, in the intricacies of long-term index numbers, particularly when administratively determined prices and exchange rates compound the difficulties of applying the usual yardsticks of static and dynamic comparative aggregate efficiency (intercountry and intertemporal). One of the most difficult questions seems to us to be that of the criteria of evaluation, the very definition of costs and benefits of a process of development which was consciously initiated and implemented by a political force pursuing definite objectives. Are the criteria for success to be the *stated* objectives ('verbally revealed preferences' of the communist leaders), for instance the Khrushchevian programme of entering the higher stage of communism by the beginning of the 1980s? Or are they to be the *imputed* ones, like the strengthening of the communist power system or the achievement of superpower status? These are not abstract academic questions, because criteria of this kind might have been used in allocation of resources to the detriment of other possible objectives. We mention them not because we are capable of assigning to them any specific weight in overall evaluation—we certainly are not—but merely because they should not be overlooked. In terms of what we have called the imputed criteria the strategy might have proven itself: after all, the world of 'real socialism' has expanded dramatically in the post World War II period, and for a long time seemed to have been securely established. But even at the time when these achievements appeared irreversible, it was not by these yardsticks that the fulfilment of the socialist promise should be measured. A rational economy, relieved of capitalist fetters, ought to perform appropriately in terms of conventional economic and welfare indicators. As mentioned before, the application of such indicators raises a great number of difficult technical issues and contentious interpretations which we do not need to consider. Nevertheless, it seems possible to sketch a general picture of the effects of the development effort undertaken in the countries of 'real socialism'; by and large this should be sufficient for our purposes.

First, over a substantial period the socialist countries have reported impressive rates of overall growth. For the half-century following the launch of the Soviet-type development strategy in 1928, the official USSR statistics claim an annual compounded rate of growth (national income = net material product) of almost 9 per cent, the war years included; American estimates of Soviet GNP more or less halve this rate, but it remains still higher than that of any major Western country except Japan.[7] By and large the pattern repeated itself in the countries of Eastern Europe, which had the following annual average rates of growth of national income (according to official figures) for the 30 years 1950–1980: Romania over 9 per cent; Bulgaria 8 per cent; Poland, GDR, and Yugoslavia around 6 per cent; and Hungary and Czechoslovakia around 5 per cent.[8] The official Chinese figure for the 1952–1981 period amounts to 6 per cent; and for the period of the first five-year plan (1952–57), when China imitated closely the Soviet model, the rate given is 9 per cent per annum. Whatever the detailed scrutiny of comparative performance, there can be no doubt that the Soviet Union has over the period in question reduced the gap dividing her from the industrialized countries of the West in terms of both per caput product and economic structure (the specific weight of industry in the economy, urbanization, and so on).[9] From this point of view the record of East European countries is less impressive when compared with other countries of Europe which started the postwar era at similar levels of development (Bulgaria, Romania, and Yugoslavia compared with Greece; Poland and Hungary with Spain; East Germany with West Germany; and Czechoslovakia with Austria). It is commonly accepted that taken as a whole the relative Czechoslovak record is particularly disappointing, apart of course from that of Poland in the wake of the crisis which has engulfed the country since the end of the 1970s. As for China, she compared well with the rest of the Asian continent in the initial period, while falling clearly behind the newly industrialized countries later on.

In general, one could say that the overall initial objectives of the Soviet-type development strategy—rapid creation or substantial expansion of the industrial base of the economy, especially with regard to extractive industries, iron and steel, and heavy engineering—have been by and large achieved. In this sense, of pushing the economy in the direction desired by the political leadership, central planning proved a workable instrument; however, it would be difficult to find specific plans actually fulfilled, not only in respect of the entire spectrum of indicators, but even with regard to the expected growth of output.

The second general conclusion is that the plans singularly and consistently failed in respect of the cost of growth. Even in narrowly economic terms—that is, without counting the enormous toll of death and human suffering in the periods when physical terror was a major component of the implementation of the Soviet-type development strategy—actual costs as a rule vastly exceeded the planned estimates and were very high by any standards. The intensity of inputs (labour, material, and capital) in relation to output in countries of 'real socialism' was substantially higher not only in the leading industrial countries but also those countries at a similar level of economic development. This is especially true of the degree of material intensity (use of energy, steel, cement, and so on in relation to national income) and of the dynamic of capital intensity in the process of growth. The Soviet rate of change of capital productivity was negative over the entire half-century, with the decline strongly pronounced in the last 25 years. The incremental capital/output ratios—the relationship between investment and the increase in national income—rose significantly in the CMEA countries over the postwar period, and on the whole faster than in Western Europe. The long-term growth of labour productivity looks more favourable, owing both to structural changes and to the Gerschenkronian 'advantage of backwardness' in the scope for imitative technical progress. But also in this area the countries of 'real socialism' lag considerably behind the West, and the scale of overmanning in industry gives rise to accusations of hiding unemployment behind factory gates.

The nature of the objectives of the Soviet-type development strategy combined with its high-cost characteristics also had wide-ranging negative consequences for *environmental issues*, which were supposed to be singularly cared for under socialism in view of its expected capacity to 'internalize externalities' (see Chapter 1). In actual fact, the arbitrary power to impose narrowly selected objectives, and to disregard long-term implications if they were seen as interfering with the chosen aims, has led in many cases to damage to the environment in countries of 'real socialism' on a scale almost unknown nowadays in developed capitalist countries. Contrary to the theoretical hypotheses, sole state ownership of the means of production proved to be more hindrance than help in preventing pollution, deforestation, and other forms of upset to the natural balance. The Janus-faced state—as the presumed protector of the environment on the one hand, and the allocator of resources and the owner of the offending enterprises on the other—found itself in a schizophrenic position, without the possibility of effective use of even the habitual means of fighting environmental abuse (fines and the like). The command system of managing the economy magnified the problem.

The third aspect of this general picture is that the high cost of growth, approximating quite often the situation of 'production for the sake of production', could not but affect adversely the dynamic of consumption. Abundant compensation had been promised to the population for the sacrifices imposed in the initial period of the steep increase in the rate of accumulation, but it never actually materialized. Even in the years between the mid 1950s and the early 1970s, when the standard of living in European socialist countries was rising rather steadily on average, the improvement was still out of proportion to the overall growth of output. All intercountry comparisons between Western and Eastern Europe show also that, in this relatively favourable period, Eastern Europe remained at a clear disadvantage as far as consumer gains from growth were concerned. In the 1970s and 1980s, when the issue of consumer satisfaction became much more sensitive politically, governments tried to shelter consumption, first by borrowing abroad (or using for this purpose of windfall profits, as in the case of the USSR), and then by reducing the share of accumulation. The effects were meagre and threatened future development because of the difficulties of compensating for reduced inflow of resources by using them more efficiently. One should not ignore the existence of some factors which may offset the disadvantages in the level and dynamic of consumption in countries of 'real socialism'. These include job security under conditions of frequent overemployment, a more equitable income distribution, and the lack of enormous wealth differentials, which some social analysts regard as guarantees against the kind of deprivation observed in rundown inner-city areas in the West, let alone in Third World slums. The reverse side of the coin is the everyday hardship of shortages and the dependence on bureaucratic, politically structured, distributional machinery in all walks of life. These remarks are intended not to provide a balance sheet of the performance of socialist countries in the field of consumption, but only to point out the link between high cost of growth and reduced potential for increasing welfare. On the other hand, the negative impact of the military burden on consumption should not be forgotten either.

Fourthly, the type of growth pursued, and the kind of modernization achieved in the USSR and Eastern Europe so far, does not augur well for further development. The slowdown of growth over the last quarter of a century has been remarkable in its scale and relentlessness. The slide for the region as a whole is interrupted during only one five-year plan period (1966–70), while in Eastern Europe outside the USSR there was a second pause in 1971–75 when these countries borrowed heavily abroad. As a rule, planners attempted to take into account the decline by planning growth rates below those actually achieved in the preceding period, but these lower plans in turn remained unfulfilled. The record of individual countries varied. East Germany (the German Democratic Republic or GDR) showed statistically the smallest deceleration and the capacity to stabilize the rate of growth at the new level. In general, however—at least until the mid 1980s—the downward trend persisted, and it would be hard to explain it by the higher degree of maturity reached by the European socialist countries. The reasons—accepted in the late 1980s with truly astonishing unanimity by both Western experts and communist leaders, in the first place Gorbachev—lie in the inability to compensate for the reduced rate at which resources can be made available by increasing their efficiency of use, or (as the widely applied slogan goes) in failing to meet the need for a changeover from 'extensive' to 'intensive' patterns of growth. These are not entirely precise terms, because they might suggest that the past Soviet and East European growth was due exclusively to the increase in the supply of factors of production, without any 'residual' (that is, growth of output per unit of combined factor input). In fact, massive additions to labour of better educated and trained people, and equally massive additions to capital of the means for technical and organizational progress (*inter alia* thanks to imitation and borrowing), must have brought some corresponding increase in total factor productivity.[10] Nevertheless, the slogan reflects the realization of the pressing necessity not merely to arrest the decline but to raise the level of efficiency compared with the past and particularly with the non-communist countries. The connection between these deficiencies and the development strategy pursued is not always accepted, at least not explicitly and not with a unanimity equal to that concerning the very existence of the short-comings. The present authors, however, belong to those who emphat-ically acknowledge this connection, subscribing to the term 'conservative modernization'[11] as a fitting designation of the outcome of the Soviet-type development strategy. This paradoxical sounding term—in relation both to the very concept of modernization and to the proclaimed revolutionary nature of the communist regimes—seems to reflect well the undeniable progress in overcoming back-wardness on the one hand, and the lack of a continuous propensity to change on the other. The missing propensity to change, to generate by the modernized economy a further momentum of its own, can be seen with particular clarity in three interrelated areas:

Technology Predominantly imitative technical progress might be under-standable for countries below the 'frontiers of technology', but at some stage should produce a spillover effect in spurring on home-grown technology and product innovations. It is this that is so rare in socialist countries, despite the substantial spending on science, the developed educational system, and the abolition of commercial secrecy, which was supposed to ensure unham-pered information flow between firms, sectors, and countries.

Structure The countries of 'real socialism' have been relatively successful in developing traditional industries. In the past these could have been rightly regarded as engines of growth, but—as with steel and a number of branches of heavy engineering—they have since lost this role; nevertheless they still retain their commanding position. However, there is not a single case of leapfrogging into frontier technologies like electronics, plastics, manmade fibres, or new pharmaceuticals; the usual picture is that of following with a time lag. Structural changes of the kind postulated above are difficult under any conditons, but the sluggishness of this process in 'real socialism' stands out; yet long-term planning was supposed to foresee and pre-empt future trends.

Foreign trade Progress in industrialization notwithstanding, the trade between socialist countries and the West bears all the marks of underdevel-opment: a predominance of primary goods in export, but of manufactures (especially with a high technology content) in import. Almost nothing has changed in this respect over time, except that the export capabilities in primary goods have diminished without a compensating rise in export potential in manufactures; this lies at the heart of the chronic balance of payments difficulties.

Is 'conservative modernization' unsatisfactory? The answer depends again on the criteria applied. From the Third World perspective, as well as that of a number of countries at what may be called an intermediate level of development, the verdict should not be absolutely negative. After all, no European socialist country (Albania excluded) belongs today to the underdeveloped category. Progress has been evident and has been coupled with a degree of social security hardly achievable elsewhere at the same or even higher levels of development. The prospects for the future are evidently not bright, although the retention of the old system need not necessarily result in economic collapse.

However, in the socialist countries themselves the prevailing mood is clearly that of profound discontent. This is particularly striking in the Soviet Union, where the affirmation of the status quo in the twilight of Brezhnev's rule has given way to Gorbachev's proclaimed policy of *perestroika*—depicted as a revolutionary change which will once again spur the economy into rapid expansion, this time sustained and based on the full use of the efficiency potential.

To what extent is this clear and increasingly open dissatisfaction with the past record of economic performance motivated by ideological concerns about the image of socialism, and to what extent by pragmatic considerations? It is hardly possible or even necessary to speculate about the relative importance of the two; they now go together perhaps more closely than ever before. The objective of catching up has not been achieved, both because socialism has failed to run as fast as expected, and because capitalism has refused to stand still. The painful ideological consequences were first manifested in replacing Khrushchev's recklessly specific promise of 'full communism' by the 'advanced socialism' formula, which in turn was being gradually watered down to an initial stage of advanced socialism and similar face-saving designations.[12] In China the XIIIth congress of the party actually went so far back as to locate the country in the initial stages of a prolonged *transition to socialism*. In sum, the realization that catching up is not a once-and-for-all but a continous contest with the distinct possibility of the gap not only remaining but even increasing, has led the official ideologists to downgrade the degree of socialist transformation accomplished. At the same time the down-to-earth pressures became stronger. Despite the successful enhancement of the Soviet position on the world scene and the preservation of communist power domestically, the deterioration in economic performance had to be recognized as a possible threat to both: the sluggishness of technical progress was in the long run perilous to the military balance, and the inability to meet rising consumer aspirations was a danger to the internal political order. From the latter point of view the warning signs in Eastern Europe, especially the Polish crisis of the 1980s, were serious enough to ring alarm bells throughout the domain of 'real socialism'.

'Conservative modernization' is thus unsatisfactory. The objective is to dynamize the economy—not, however, by a rapid rise in the burden of accumulation, but by very substantial improvements in factor productivity through innovations, higher quality, a reduction in input/output ratios, a restructuring in favour of modern industries and technologies, and a switch from primary goods to manufactures in exports to the West. The emphasis is also on balanced development, on matching supply and demand both within the production sphere and in consumption, as against the high selectivity of the past.

The relevance of identifying deficiencies and formulating a programme of rectification should not be underestimated, particularly in a country like the Soviet Union where the ruling elite was for such a long time and so doggedly presenting a rosy picture to the outside world that it must even have fallen victim to self-deception. Nevertheless, the crucial question is that of implementation, the more so that the USSR and the East European countries have tried to extricate themselves from the 'extensive pattern' of running the economy for decades—in vain. The 'new course' launched shortly after Stalin's death in 1953 can be regarded as the first attempt of this kind. It heralded the policy of lessening the tautness of the plans and lifting the position of the hitherto neglected sectors (agriculture, consumer goods, and services, as well as science-based industries) in resource allocation. The rate of investment was reduced not only for the sake of consumption but also in order to increase efficiency by improving the supply situation and curtailing the number of construction projects, which lengthened gestation periods. Greater attention to consumer interests was to serve efficiency too by providing the base for strengthening incentives. Although a considerable portion of this reallocation was later reversed, the general line of economic policies in the post-Stalin period differed substantially from the past: the investment burden never again rose to its previous heights; agriculture (and to some extent light industry) increased its share in resource allocation; and real incomes grew, albeit slowly. Nonetheless, the tensions in the economy persisted, and the expected intensification of development failed to materialize. Another attempt at dynamization failed in the 1970s, when several countries embarked on a policy of 'import-led growth'. A massive injection of extra resources, including Western technology, acquired on credit or—in the Soviet case—with the windfall profits from energy exports, not only failed to counter-balance the inherent weaknesses of the socialist economics but actually exposed them more severely.

The experience of the persistent failures to improve the working of the economy by various policy changes has corroborated the point made earlier by a number of economists, and developed in a particularly clear and comprehensive way by the Hungarian scholar Janos Kornai,[13] that the reasons for the lack of success were *systemic*. It was the system of functioning of the economy, the economic mechanism, which reproduced tensions at any level of tautness of the plans, caused waste of resources, and consequently barred the way to a rise in living standards. By the mid 1980s, more or less three decades after it was first formulated as a programme of economic reform, the need for radical change in the economic system of 'real socialism' became accepted by most communist leaderships, including those of the two giants, the USSR and China. This makes it necessary for us to go back and to examine the nature of the economic system which has dominated 'real socialism' throughout its existence hitherto.

4

The Command System

We are concerned mainly with the economic system of 'real social-ism'. However, before we turn to it a brief discussion of a few more general questions is in order.

The survey of the Marxist claim to the economic rationality of Socialism in Chapter 1 should have made explicit that in this vision a fundamental change in the economic behaviour of the members of the society has been assumed. *Homo oeconomicus* has been expected to blend with *Homo socialis* on the basis of ownership of the means of production being perceived as genuinely common, and hence erasing the distinction between principals and agents; rivalry is to be replaced by a spirit of sharing and cooperation. Although it has been accepted that the overcoming of the alienation of labour cannot be complete at the outset of the new era, and therefore that distribution according to work will be unavoidable for some time in order fully to bring together individual and social interests, the intrinsic foundations of a *new motivation syndrome* would be in place. This conviction has evidently been linked with the maturity conditions of the transition to socialism, in both a material and a cultural sense, the latter—to use Gramsci's term—reflected in the proletarian 'cultural hegemony'.

Several thick layers of divergence separate this image from the realities of 'real socialism'. First, the idealized concept of the 'new man' was evidently utopian under any circumstances. Secondly, 'real socialism' emerged under conditions of immaturity, which according to the Marxist theory itself—regardless of the view on the legitimacy of socialist revolution—could not generate the new attitudes for a long time to come. Thirdly, even in cases of indigenous revolutions, at least a substantial minority (and in Russia, judging by the results of the election to the Constituent Assembly, probably a majority) opposed the new regime, while in Eastern Europe it was received with deep hostility as not only unwanted in itself but in addition imposed from outside. Fourthly, with all political pluralism wiped out, state power was monopolized in the hands of the Communist Party, which could not be but inimical to the idea of state ownership as a common good. Fifthly, despite all this the mono-party, or rather its ruling elite, pushed forward with (by and large) the preconceived design, alienating people even further and resorting even more to coercion. We will not elaborate on these telegraphically formulated points, but their enumeration should help us to appreciate the gulf between the assumed and the true motivational structure. This is not to say that the expected socialist attitudes were completely absent; however, they certainly did not dominate, and moreover they diminished rather than increased over time.

The realization of the discrepancy between expectations and reality in this respect manifested itself in practical political terms for the first time in the history of 'real socialism' during the turnabout from 'war communism' to the famous 'new economic policy' (NEP) in 1921. Lenin was emphatic in admitting that to rely solely on enthusiasm in organizing production and distribution on communist principles was a mistake, and that personal material interest and economic accountability (*khozraschet*) must play a paramount role.[1] Material incentives, linked directly or indirectly to the operation of the market, as well as a relatively broad scope for private economic activity, were the hallmarks of the NEP, repeated in one way or another in all countries of 'real socialism' in the initial period of their post-revolutionary existence. However, again in all these countries alike, after a few years the mixed economy with substantial market regulation was replaced by that system of functioning of the economy—if not identical, then at least very similiar—widely known as the *command system* (one of the present authors used the term 'centralistic system'[2]). The correspondence in time betwen this change in economic mechanism and the embarkation on the Soviet-type development strategy raised the question of interconnection—a subject of unending debates among students of the history of 'real socialism'.

The complexities of the interaction between the crash industrialization policy and the command system of functioning of the economy are multiplied by the interference of the ideological allegiance to the Marxist design of socialism/communism as a directly planned marketless economy.[3] Of course, neither the 'war communism' of 1918–20, nor the end to the NEP by collectivization of agriculture, elimination of the private sector, and centralization of economic management in the Soviet Union, as well as by analogous policies in other countries, can be explained by ideological considerations alone—but the role of the vision was considerable. It generated among the party faithful what may be called a high propensity to embrace every move towards comprehensive state control as a step in the right direction: the more nationalization and centralization, the more socialism. It pushed the actual measures beyond what might be regarded as justified on the pragmatic grounds of the adopted policies, and made them last longer; it instilled the perception of any step in the opposite direction (greater scope for market coordination, incentives, non-state-controlled economic activity, and so on) as a regrettable temporary concession, an enforced retreat which was to be stopped at the first opportunity. Thus the ideological factor must be seen as at least in part responsible for the fact that no effort was made at the time to safeguard some scope for individual interests and activity, which need not necessarily be eliminated even during a massive investment drive undertaken by government within the framework of an overall macroeconomic plan.

Nevertheless, while keeping in mind the impact of the ideology, the close link between the Soviet-type development strategy and the system of functioning of the economy cannot be overlooked. This strategy had to rely on the state *forcing* the allocation of material and human resources in accordance with the objectives set and the path chosen to achieve them. Not only could the internalization of state policies by the population not be counted upon, but also the general conditions and scope for material incentives had become radically different from those familiar in the past. By the change in general *conditions* we mean the elimination of the aggregate effective demand constraint as a result of the expansive growth policy and various systemic factors. Instead of being demand determined, the economy became supply determined. This freed it of the absurdity (see Chapter 1) of the coexistence of excess capital and labour with unsatisfied needs, but at the same time weakened to the point of disappearance the incentives deriving from the struggle to find a market for products and factors of production. With growing shortages this soon led to a complete dominance of the supplier over the consumer and user of factors of production. By the change in *scope* for material incentives we mean primarily the limitations deriving from the paucity of the consumer goods on offer, resulting frequently in formal or informal rationing and a weakening of the stimuli for voluntary savings by the population.

All in all, whether from the 'enthusiasm end' or from the 'incentive end', no room for spontaneous activity of individuals or groups was left in the process. Thus it was not enough for the state to control and to regulate the behaviour of economic units, as it were, from outside.

The state had to become *the* economic actor itself, both on the macroscale and on the microscale, so as to secure the generation and collection of savings, to invest, to produce, and to distribute. Moreover, the monopolization by the state of economic decisions related to the development strategy did not simply mean the creation of a mega-entrepreneur (USSR Inc., as it was sometimes called in Western literature). Economic power became intertwined with political and police power, and although the communist mono-archy was firmly in place from the very onset of 'real socialism', and hence cannot be simply derived from the crash industrialization policy, the iron heel was heaviest in the course of this policy, and the subordination of individual preferences to the superior preferences of the state was at its peak. In this sense, we think that the term *coercive model*[4] is an appropriate designation of the implementation mechanism of the Soviet-type development strategy, even when it does not reach such extremes of terror as during the Soviet collectivization drive and the late 1930s purges, or as it did throughout Eastern Europe under the Stalinist regime. The command system is thus the narrower economic component of the coercive model.

The command system has been described so many times and in such detail in the economic literature that we feel free to dispense with an attempt to present a complete picture. In what follows we discuss it from two viewpoints only: first, how it relates to the modernization strategy; and secondly, how it has contributed to the conservatism of the outcome.

In Chapter 3, our summary exposition of the development strategy concentrated on three main points: rapid growth through a steep rise in the rate of accumulation; selective growth; and output and employment maximization. How instrumental was the command system in attaining these tasks?

Enforcement of the desired rate of accumulation proceeded through strict control over the 'terms of trade' between the state as an integrated producer, employer, and seller on the one side, and the households on the other side. (In all countries of 'real socialism' there had been remnants of a private sector, which in one case, that of Polish agriculture, was even of substantial significance for the economy; but we omit the matter here.) The economic interaction between the state and the households was conducted (in principle) through the market: households received money income from work in the state sector, and spent it on goods and services sold by the state sector (*kolkhozi* are treated as part of the state sector, and the subsistence component of the economy is disregarded). The mechanism of forced savings consisted of administrative regulation of these market or quasi-market relations through determination of prices and wages, combined with direct physical controls in particularly sensitive areas, such as the long-surviving system of the extraction of agricultural produce by way of compulsory deliveries at nominal prices. To some extent the aggregate labour supply too was forced to rise, not only through economic pressure (low levels of income requiring more than one earner in the family), but also through administrative regulation of the duty to work and the widespread use of manifold forms of compulsion. The price mechanism remained operative in most areas of allocation of consumer goods: the peasant market, with varying degrees of freedom, and state retail trade. In the latter, prices were supposed to balance supply and demand to provide freedom of choice (but not consumer sovereignty, because market signals were not transmitted automatically to the producers). However, in practice open or disguised rationing and queueing prevailed, because even under the political conditions of mono-archy it is difficult to bring about the desired rate of surplus by effective control of money incomes alone. Thus, as observed earlier, the toll was taken very often through hidden and repressed inflation.

Selective development was to be achieved by physical allocation of resources to chosen users. This required detailed planning of the output of the supplying units, including the product mix, the time sequence, and the norms of outlay per unit of effect (individual input/output coefficients). The supply and demand sides were to be balanced by the planners in the process of adjustment of output and input schedules. Distribution in physical terms, that is rationing, was supposed to follow the prescribed schedule through an organizational hierarchy of economic management; vertical flows were addressed from above to the next lower administrative unit, while horizontal relations between the final suppliers and users remained purely technical. As for allocation of labour, the principle of free choice of occupation was maintained in European socialist countries, and hence the wage mechanism retained some significance in this respect. However, deviations from the principle were widespread: quasi-voluntary mobilizations; administrative assignments, particularly of graduates of universities and vocational schools; restrictions on the movement of the population (especially severe and long-lasting with regard to the Soviet *kolkhoz* peasantry); and straightforward forced labour of conscripts, prisoners, and labour camp inmates. In China practically all vestiges of the labour market were suppressed.

Output maximization was pursued through the system of obligatory plan targets; the relationship between the planned and the actual magnitude was the main success indicator for all levels of organizational hierarchy, from the lowest production unit up to the ministry. The feeding mechanism, both with regard to supply of physical factors of production and in financial terms, was geared to plan fulfilment. Cost calculations and profit-and-loss accounts were obviously there, but they followed physical output and allocation decisions, serving at the most an *ex post* control function. Thus within the state sector money played only a passive role, which meant that the units called enterprises were under a 'soft budget constraint',[5] that is they would not be prevented by unfavourable financial results from producing the planned output and maintaining employment. In addition, the domestic economy was insulated from external influence by the state monopoly of foreign trade, operating a strict and comprehensive export/import plan and neutralizing the effect of external profits or losses on domestic enterprises by individual taxation and subsidies ('price equalization mechanism').

This rough sketch of the principles of the command system leaves out not only details and country-specific elements, but also its evolution over time. Nevertheless the outline seems sufficient to show the links between the system of functioning and the rapid industrialization strategy—not perhaps in the absolute sense that no other options were available (particularly in Eastern Europe), but that this choice was the most likely considering jointly the impact of the strategy, the existing ideological framework, the political system, and the state of knowledge about planning in general.

Now let us turn to the second part of the question: in what way has the command system contributed to the conservatism of the modernization in 'real socialism'?[6]

As indicated earlier, the basic method of planning under a command system is the method of material balances, which amounts to separately collating and making compatible the rows and columns of an input/output table. However, as the number of items to be considered reaches many hundreds of thousands, it proves hardly possible to compile a comprehensively consistent plan based on individual material balances. As a result plans are worked out which, although very detailed, are inconsistent and therefore *a priori* incapable of being fulfilled in their totality. Construction of plans which cannot be fulfilled as a whole may be called the 'planning paradox' of the centrally planned economies.[7] Theoretically the solution to this problem could be found in the input/output technique by inverting Leontief's matrix, which would lead to a consistent set of intermediate products. However, the statistically obtainable input/output tables contain data that are too highly aggregated; and information regarding detailed technical coefficients and available primary production factors either does not reach the planning centre at all, or reaches it late and in distorted form. An additional technical problem—unrealistically assuming the availability of sufficiently detailed information—would be the inversion of such a highly disaggregated matrix. Under these conditions some experts regard the primitive 'method of balances' as superior to sophisticated input/output techniques, because it at least allows the achievement of partial consistency of the plans.[8]

Inconsistent plans cannot be fulfilled in their totality by definition, and yet they are made obligatory under a command system. The paradox does not end here, however. The seldom explicit but nevertheless actual premise underlying the obligatory character of the plans is that of full controllability of economic processes. In reality the nature of the economic processes is stochastic, which means that to foresee all the factors influencing economic processes is impossible. Moreover, the matter cannot be reduced to planning mistakes or similar points; unforeseeable reactions of the economic actors to unexpected events must be included as well. A harmonious development of interdependent stochastic processes therefore requires of the economic actors a flexibility of behaviour which comes into conflict with the obligatory character of the plan.[9]

On top of the question of consistency is the problem of efficiency in the course of the plan construction. At stake is the maximization of the effect of the application of the given factors of production, and this depends on the appropriate choice of technical coefficients in the production of every good. The choice of techniques plays a particularly important part in the creation of new production capacities. Another efficiency problem arises in connection with foreign trade. The consistency element here requires the balancing of imports by exports, but this is obviously insufficient from the point of view of efficiency because of the possibility of substitution of imports by domestic production and of opportunities to vary the composition of exports. Finally, there is the problem of the optimal structure of output in general and of such subaggregates as consumer goods and investment. It is self-evident that, in order to make efficient choices, precise and flexible information as to the costs and effects of each variant is indispensable.

As we have seen in Chapter 1, the Marxist vision of socialism is concerned only with the removal of social impediments to rational allocation; it ignores what at the time might have seemed a purely technical question of commensurate valuation of the costs and effects of alternative actions, in yardsticks which reflect their social relevance and remain as feasible independent parameters of choice for the decision-makers. The role of such information carriers in a market economy is performed better or worse by prices, broadly defined to include wages, interest rates, and rents. Postulating abolition of the market, Marxist theory failed to provide socialism with a viable method of generating prices, either in the narrow sense of exchange relations between goods or in the wider sense of indicators of the alternatives of choice. The command system has hardly made up this handicap. It has to use prices within the state economy as a means of aggregation or control, but because of the dominance of physical planning, the passive role of money, and hence the low responsiveness to prices of the managers of nationalized enterprises, the role of prices in efficiency calculations is minimal. Paradoxically enough, taking into account the quality of prices under the command system—their failure to reflect many elements of social costs (capital, natural resources) and supply demand conditions, the bureaucratic way they were determined, and so on—to use them widely in the decision-making process might have been even less rational. So-called shadow prices, derived (as a 'dual') from the established or considered physical structure by computation, could at least have provided the planners with valuations consistent with their own prior choices. However, even apart from technical problems similar to those of application of input/output methodology, shadow prices would be of little help in determining the efficient physical structure itself. Thus the only reliable points of reference left to the planners for comparing economic alternatives are prices on the capitalist world market. They too, however, have seldom been used to their full potential in domestic pricing practice. Considering the fact that world market prices are being applied—at least in principle—in intra-Comecon trade, the reason for this could hardly have been ideological; perhaps the planners' constant grappling for the elusive consistency makes them altogether less sensitive to the efficiency problems of their plans. The informational deficiencies connected with price distortions are augmented by the impact of the political system: when macrodecisions of great complexity and with substantial externalities have to be made, which go beyond the capacity of the market, the mono-archy engenders another information barrier preventing genuine choice among the options available.

The informational weaknesses of the command system interact with weakness of incentives. We have already mentioned the lack of competitive incentives and the fragility of those linked to consumers' choice. To compensate for this a variety of specially designed incentive schemes has been tried throughout the entire period of operation of the command system—both for workers (piece-rate wage schemes were at one time extended in countries of 'real socialism' to a degree unknown elsewhere) and for the managers. However, the very logic of the command system demands that incentives should be geared to plan fulfilment; this, intertwined with the information barriers, has become the main source of deformation. The managers' interest in plan fulfilment is to be fostered both by immediate financial rewards and by their general career prospects. The interest of rank-and-file employees is linked to plan fulfilment less directly (the basic wage and salary structure is determined independently), but the link is there because the overall wage bill is related in some way to plan filfilment, and various individual bonuses in cash and in kind, as well as collective benefits, are contingent upon it. The seeming simplicity of such incentive schemes disappears as soon as one takes into account the multiplicity of the objectives contained in the plan (quantity, quality, product mix, costs, and so on), and the obvious likelihood of conflicts between them. In the long history of the command system there has been no substantial experience (although there were abortive attempts) of applying *ex ante* relative weights to particular objectives in order to arrive at a sort of aggregate indicator, with trade-offs reflecting macrovaluations known in advance to enterprise management. These difficulties are multiplied by what is frequently termed the plan pressure. It has been assumed that targets and norms for the use of resources ought to be taut in order to mobilize fully the existing potential. The plan pressure is to provide a kind of substitute for the lack of competitive pressure. The notorious method of 'planning from the achieved level' (the so-called 'ratchet principle') means that fulfilment of a target leads almost automatically to an increase for the next planning period.

Under the circumstances, an informal managerial behaviour pattern has evolved that is far removed from the one expected in the Marxist vision of socialism. The main features of this pattern can conveniently be arranged into three groups: priority adjustment, the peculiar 'minimax' strategy, and change aversion.[10] Priority adjustment consists of choosing among the conflicting objectives of the plan those promising the highest performance from the enterprise, regardless of the consequences for society as a whole. Usually the output indicator becomes the overriding concern, which is again a reflection of the logic of the system. As the aggregate volume of output can seldom be measured in physical terms, plan targets are as a rule expressed in a value of production, such as gross, net, or sold; this allows manipulation of the product mix so as to fulfil the overall target with less of the 'difficult' and more of the 'easy' items. The 'easy' products are those priced beneficially in relation to the required effort, and not necessarily those in greatest demand. From the same point of view the quality aspect, hard to capture precisely, is pushed down to the lowest level of acceptability. Some priorities are explicitly imposed on the producers from above, among other things the order in which various categories of recipients of output—enterprises, industries, regions—are to be supplied. The existence of such priority lists is in itself evidence of the inconsistency of the plans, an admission that parts of them are being regarded as unfulfillable. This differentiated attitude of the planners themselves to the relevance of particular indicators could not but encourage lower-level management to adjust priorities according to their own criteria.

The essence of the 'minimax' strategy peculiar to the command system is to find ways to minimize the plan targets and simultaneously to maximize the planned allocation of resources. Taking advantage of the imperfection of the information available to the central planners, each level of the economic administration—from plant managers to industrial ministers—tries to hide capacities and to inflate the indents for inputs in order to reduce the plan pressure. In a specific manner this applies to wages as well: concerned not with financial results in an absolute sense but at most with the limits set by the plan ('soft budget constraint'), enterprises and industries strive to obtain during the planning process as high a wage bill and as favourable wage rates in relation to targets as possible. As insurance from the consequences of irregular and incomplete deliveries of inputs, the widespread hoarding of raw materials, intermediate goods, and components becomes the rule, boosting inventories in one place at the expense of shortage elsewhere, and hence undermining the very idea of cost-effectiveness of planned coordination on the macros-cale. Hoarding applies to labour as well (for a variety of reasons), contributing substantially to overmanning, which then becomes an increasingly important factor in the employment situation; even at times of contraction of investment and explicit efforts to reduce employment planning authorities are faced with stable or growing demand for labour.

The aversion to change, as innovations in both the methods of production and the products themselves, stems from the same motivation. The process of preparing and introducing an innovation usually requires considerable effort, which may not be sufficiently reflected in the criteria of evaluation that directly interest the unit concerned. The risk of outright failure of the intended innovation and the possible adverse impact on current output is the primary consideration; however, success may not pay off either, because of the ratchet principle: the new process or the new product is as a rule included in the next plan, raising the threshold from which further progress is counted and remunerated. 'More of the same' thus becomes the rational rule of behaviour under these peculiar circumstances. In addition, whereas genuine innovations may often harm the direct interests of an enterprise, the special incentives introduced from above to counter the aversion to change actually spur the propensity to spurious innovations. This is especially true of novel products entitled to fetch higher official prices; the practice of presenting marginally altered goods as new ones is widely used as a means of inflating the quantitative indicators of plan fulfilment. The phenomenon of bogus new products—which, apart from consumer goods, probably occur most in engineering—is apparently one of the main factors in overestimation of the rates of growth of national income and industrial output in countries of 'real socialism'. It should also be clear, we think, that all these features of the command system contribute substantially to the failure of 'real socialism' to meet the expectations of internalization of externalities in respect of the environment (see Chapter 3).

We would like to avoid the impression that the motivation and behaviour sketched above are omnipresent; there are people who are ideologically motivated, as well as many more who are simply keen to do their work properly. However, they have to act not in accordance with the true incentive pattern generated by the system, but against it. In the long run this is inevitably a lost battle, with a diminishing number of fighters and relentlessly growing frustration. It is also worth remembering that, so far, we have been discussing almost exclusively the implications of the economic system in the narrow sense, only occasionally mentioning the economic consequences of the political and police factor. Needless to say, the latter not only has nipped in the bud any initial hopes of popular participation in or influence on decision-making, thus making hollow the promise of disalienation, but also has paralysed initiative, boldness, and innovativeness through the fear of being declared and punished as wrecker, saboteur, and enemy of the people, quite often to cover up the failures of the system and the policies adopted. A major factor strengthening these attitudes is the *nomenklatura* system of selection to positions of responsibility, which promotes the obedient followers of the party line in preference to the independent, daring, and imaginative.

To sum up, it seems that the thesis of the twin role of the command system—as an instrument both of the Soviet-type modernization strategy and of its inbred conservatism—can be upheld. It should also be apparent from our discussion that we do not share the view of the contrasting time-specific valuation of the command system—as fully fitting the period of 'extensive growth', and only later disclosing its weaknesses. In our opinion this view is not sustainable, either on logical grounds (why should a capital-wasting system be appropriate in a period of greatest capital shortage?) or on the historical evidence of early attempts to do away with the command system, and of countries at relatively very low levels of economic development being virtually forced to change by the disastrous results of the old economic mechanism (China, and later even more strikingly Vietnam). The refutation of the 'everything right in its time' position (a close relative of the political syndrome of the Communist Party being always right) is not tantamount to denial of the growing inadequacy of the command system with the increasing complexity of the economy, which must have been a factor in the learning process leading the ruling elites in countries of 'real socialism' towards the recognition of the urgency of reform.

The lesson from the experience of the socialist economies—the need to reform the system—is therefore not surprising. Nor is the direction of reform unexpected. In the most general terms it is to make use—in one way or another—of the market mechanism which is at the core of the attempted change. Thus what has to be done next in this book is to examine the process of the market-oriented reforms in countries of 'real socialism'. It seems advisable to precede this examination, however, with a discussion of some of the theoretical problems of 'market socialism'.

PART III

Market Socialism—the Problems So Far

5

The Theoretical Response to Challenge

The vision of the future socialist economy as free of the evils of the market was already tarnished by the end of the nineteenth century, particularly with the emergence of the revisionist strain in Marxism associated with the name of Eduard Bernstein. After World War I and the Russian Revolution of 1917, the orthodox Marxists within what has become known as the social-democratic wing of socialism (in contrast to the communist one), like Karl Kautsky and Otto Bauer, also began to recognize the relevance of the market for the operation of a socialist economy. As for the communist ideology, basic elements of the marketless concept of socialism remained embodied in the programme documents; these presented any utilization of the market mechanism as a temporary concession only, to be justified mainly by the immaturity of the socio-economic conditions, which required a longer transition period between capitalism and socialism, especially in underdeveloped countries with a dominant peasant agriculture and other types of 'petty commodity production'.[1]

The Soviet academic debates on the relationship between socialism and the market (or the plan and the market) in the 1920s were conducted within the confines of this ideology, although certain indirect evidence indicated that some of the economists posthumously rehabilitated in 1987 (Bazarov, Groman, Kondratiev) attempted to cross the imposed boundary.[2] At the end of the 1920s all debates stopped, to re-emerge in the communist world with various degrees of openness and consistency only after Stalin's death. In contrast, the debate in the West developed into the theoretically and politically wide-ranging subject of economic calculation under socialism. It received its impetus from a 1920 article by Ludwig von Mises, who denied the possibility of any kind of rational economic calculation under socialism because of the elimination of private ownership of the means of production and hence the lack of a genuine market for producer goods. Refutation of this view was undertaken by a number of economists, predominantly—but not exclusively—attached to the socialist idea. Probably the best known of these attempts was that of

Oskar Lange who wrote his celebrated essay 'On the Economic Theory of Socialism' after the republication in 1935 of Mises's original piece by Friedrich A. von Hayek, who rekindled the argument. Similar ideas had been developed in the same period in a series of articles by Abba Lerner, and so there arose the designation 'Lange-Lerner solution'; however, in a major book *Economics of Control* (published a few years later) Lerner actually left the 'market socialist' camp, as he ceased to link the application of his 'rule' with the dominance of public ownership of the means of production.[3] We shall discuss the theoretical problems of market socialism by and large in the context of the Lange versus Mises/Hayek controversy, which has acquired a lasting place in the history of economic thought and provides a useful introduction to the conceptual aspects of economic reforms in countries of 'real socialism'.

Oskar Lange was a radical socialist and a convinced Marxist, but he perceived Marxian economics as a broad theory of historical evolution of economic life, and hardly as a guide to the allocation of resources. This he made explicit with particular emphasis at the very time of entering the debate with Mises and Hayek. In an article published in 1935, 'Marxian Economics and Modern Economics Theory', expounded the view that 'clearly the relative merits of Marxian economics and of modern "bourgeois" [his own quotation marks—in itself a significant sign] economic theory belong to different "ranges".' Then in a footnote he referred directly to what we would now call the problems of 'real socialism': 'It is obvious that Marshallian economics offers more for the current administration of the economic system of Soviet Russia than Marxian economics does, though the latter is surely the more effective basis for anticipating the future of capitalism.'[4] The awareness of this position of Lange is important for our discussion, because it helps to understand that in the economic calculation debate he represents not so much (if at all) Marxism as neoclassical economics against the 'Austrian school'.

Most accounts of the debate, including the distinguished contributions by Abram Bergson,[5] accept that Mises's theoretical proposition had actually been proved wrong even before the debate started. Already in 1908 the Italian economist Enrico Barone had shown that, *ceteris paribus*, the theoretical solution to the problem of efficient allocation of resources is independent of the system of ownership of factors of production; what is necessary is to find a set of appropriate prices. However, though theoretically conceivable, the task is impossible in practice because of the unfeasibility of deriving the indispensable prices from many millions of simultaneous equations. According to the prevailing interpretation, Hayek acknowledged the point and ascribed to Mises the proposition not of the theoretical but of the practical incompatibility of socialism with rational economic calculation; thus Hayek's (and Lionel Robbins') position was presented as a retreat from the more extreme stance of Mises. We shall not dwell on the problem of correctness of this interpretation. What is relevant for getting the right focus on Lange's model is the straightforward way Hayek's challenge was formulated: can socialism be efficient in the sense of improving on, or at least not worsening, the productive efficiency of capitalism? Lange answered this question with a determined 'yes', proposing what he regarded as a practical solution to the problem of finding the appropriate prices: a trial-and-error empirical procedure conducted by the central planning authority. This is what the concept which became known as the 'market socialist' (Lange himself rarely used the term) or the 'competitive' solution actually boils down to. The acceptance of this answer underlies the widespread view of the debate as having shown that market socialism is capable of the same allocative efficiency as capitalism, and that therefore economic theory alone can hardly settle the big controversy over the relative merits of the two socio-economic orders.

Let us examine Lange's model of market socialism somewhat more closely, not merely to check the validity of the view that it successfully refutes the Austrian school's challenge to socialism, but also to establish whether or to what extent it can be regarded as a guide or at least an inspiration for the reforms in 'real socialism'.

Efficiency of allocation, in terms of standard Western economic theory, is usually understood as the simultaneous fulfilment of the following conditions: distributive optimum, productive maximum, and optimal composition (mix) of output. The attainment of the distributive optimum requires that the marginal rates of substitution be equal for each pair of consumer goods for all consumers. The productive maximum is analogously reached when the marginal rates of technical substitution are equal for each pair of productive factors for all producers. For the optimal composition of output, the marginal rates of substitution for each pair of consumer goods must equal the marginal rates of transformation for the same pair of goods. In the state of attained efficient allocation of resources, no welfare position of any individual can be improved without impairing the welfare position of another individual (the so-called 'Pareto optimum').

The problem of efficient allocation is the main focus of neoclassical economics. According to this school, under conditions of perfect competition (and without increasing returns to scale) the capitalist economy would secure the attainment of the optimal state. Under perfect competition, prices for all consumer goods are equal for all consumers, who maximize utility by adjusting the marginal rate of substitution for each pair of goods and services to the given (inverse) price ratio; the resultant of their separate actions would be the distributive optimum. Analogously, under perfect competition, prices of production factors are equal for all producers, who, minimizing the cost of each given quantity of output, adjust the marginal rate of technical substitution to the given (inverse) price ratio of production factors; the resultant would be the productive maximum. Finally, under perfect competition the producers behave as quantity adjusters: in order to maximize profit they expand output up to the point where the (increasing) marginal costs equal the unit price of output; the resultant would be the optimal composition of output. In this way perfect competition is supposed to lead to the state of general equilibrium in the economy.

One of the paths allegedly leading to this state was described by Walras.[6] An auctioneer finds the equilibrium prices for all goods and factors of production in a trial-and-error or *tâtonnement* process: he calls out prices, which are passively accepted by the economic actors, who accordingly formulate their individual supply and demand quotas. These intended supply and demand magnitudes are then transmitted to the auctioneer, aggregated, and tested for consistency; in the case of inconsistency, new prices are called out. The procedure is repeated until the general equilibrium is found. Then—and only then—the actual transactions are made.

Lange's solution follows essentially the Walrasian model. The core of this solution consists of efficient allocation of goods within the sphere of production. In this sphere there are two categories of economic actors: the enterprise (firm) managers and the industry managers ('captains of industry'). The enterprise managers have to follow three rules: (1) to accept the prices as parameters, that is to behave as price takers and quantity adjusters only; (2) to calculate short-term marginal costs for the enterprise output, while finding the minimum cost combination for each alternative level of output; and (3) to produce that volume of output at which marginal costs equal price. The 'captains of industry' are under the same set of rules, with the differences that for them the relevant cost curve is the long-term marginal cost curve for the sector (branch) as a whole, and that their decisions concern the expansion or contraction of productive capacities (including the creation or closure of enterprises) of the sector in question. The central planning organ (the central planning board or CPB in Lange's essay) functions like the Walrasian auctioneer: it tests prices in a trial-and-error process until supply and demand in all markets for producer goods become equal. In addition the CPB has two functions beyond that of an auctioneer: (1) the determination of the volume of investment in the economy, that is of the supply of investment goods and of the rate of interest which will adjust demand to this supply in particular sectors; and (2) the distribution of the social dividend, that is of the surplus of net revenues of the nationalized enterprises over their investment outlays (and possibly collective consumption), according to criteria independent of remuneration for work.

These are the permanent elements of Lange's solution. There are also supplementary components which make it possible to distinguish between three models—the main and two secondary. The main model has two genuine markets—for consumer goods and labour—where prices and wage rates have market-clearing properties and can be used by the producers as relative scarcity indicators. The first secondary model retains the principle of free choice of consumer goods, but not that of consumer sovereignty, by differentiating between the market prices of consumer goods and the accounting prices which are to be taken as parameters by the producers; the accounting prices and hence the composition of the consumer goods' output reflect under these conditions the preferences of the central planners and not those of the consumers. The other secondary model eliminates the market for consumer goods and labour altogether, relying instead on direct instructions (rationing) to households in their role both as units of consumption and as suppliers of labour; the accounting prices of consumer goods and labour services are however still needed, as they reflect the preferences of the central planning authorities. With these accounting prices the system remains efficient, provided the rules of the game in the production sphere are followed.

In Lange's view, his system not only satisfied the standard efficiency criteria but also promised to be superior to capitalism, among other things because of the more welfare-generating principles of distribution, as well as of the ability to take into consideration externalities and to intensify technical progress; the support that can be found in his essay for the last two assertions is probably the weakest.

We shall discuss Lange's model from two main aspects. One is its consistency; the other is whether the Walrasian approach, which Lange imitates, deals effectively with the Mises/Hayek challenge. As far as the internal consistency of the model is concerned, in our opinion Lange succeeded in showing that a central planning authority can take over the function of an auctioneer and similarly arrive at an efficient allocation of resources. This can be regarded as an important contribution to the theory of general equilibrium in the sense that market socialism may provide an alternative to perfect competition.[7] In both cases the problem is actually the same: to find those prices of all goods and production factors which would secure equilibrium in all markets. However, an important difference between the Walrasian concept of the auctioneer and Lange's concept of the functions of the central planner must be kept in mind. The Walrasian theory is a piece of *positive* economics in that it attempts to *describe* the way a capitalist economy operates; by contrast, Lange's model is intentionally *normative*, in that it tries to *prescribe* the rules which should govern the operation of market socialism. The dangers of a mistaken normative theory can, obviously, be much greater than those of a positive one. Take for instance the questions of the existence or of the stability of general equilibrium. If the general equilibrium position does not exist, let us say owing to increasing returns to scale of production, the activities of the central planner would fail to have effect, as one cannot find something which is not there.[8] In the case where general equilibrium exists but is of an unstable nature, the CPB would run into another kind of difficulty. Unlike under the Walrasian auctioneer's regime, in market socialism transactions are effected also at incorrect ('false') prices, which in itself may undermine the stability of an equilibrium or make it unattainable. The consistency of Lange's model would be even more strongly disputed by the 'new capital theory' school (based on Sraffa's works), which denies any validity to neoclassical concepts outside the narrow confines of given resources.[9] However, leaving aside the purely theoretical problems of consistency, in our opinion the most important gap in the model is the omission of the problem of *motivation* of the economic actors, both central planners and managers. The CPB is presented as an embodiment of unity, public interest, and pure reason; its only concern is to implement the rules of market socialism—to adjust prices in order to avoid shortages or gluts—without using its enormous power for any other purpose. The same goes for the managers, who are expected to comply with the rules unswervingly and precisely, without displaying the slightest signs of self-interest. It seems, therefore, that the consistency of Lange's model, as presented in the essay in question, can be salvaged only by ascribing to it an implicit assumption, in the orthodox Marxist tradition discussed in Chapter 1, of elimination under socialism of conflicts of interest, as well as of all that hampers the full and strict implementation of any rules promulgated.[10]

The second part of our discussion of the model of market socialism—whether it deals effectively with the Mises/Hayek challenge—must start with a look at the differences between the Walrasian and the Austrian theoretical perceptions of the way a market economy operates. Lange replied to the challenge by presenting an essentially Walrasian system without the capitalists. But what if the challenge was actually not Walrasian at all, and the neoclassical approach was erroneous for any type of market economy? This is the question posed recently by new students of the old economic calculation debate; their answer amounts often to a complete revision of the standard picture of the outcome of the debate.[11]

The neoclassical theory, and consequently the market socialist model considered here, takes the *tâtonnement* mechanism with the auctioneer as a justified abstract generalization of an actual process occurring in a market economy. However, whereas such emphasis is placed on the auctioneer, whose concrete prototype can hardly be found in the real world, the Walrasian model overlooks the true central figure of the capitalist system, namely the entrepreneur *sensu stricto*. Formally there are entrepreneurs in the Walrasian model, but they behave like robots, minimizing costs or maximizing profits with the data given. Their behaviour is that of pure optimizers operating in the framework of exclusively passive competition, reduced to reactive adjustment of positions to an exogenous change. This can scarcely be a legitimate generalization of competition, which in reality is a constant struggle affecting the data themselves. It is here that the static approach of the general equilibrium theory becomes particularly pronounced, contrary to the actual dynamics of a capitalist economy.

True, Schumpeter—who elevated the entrepreneur to the role of the main propeller of economic development—came to the conclusion (see Chapter 1) that mature capitalism makes the entrepreneurial function obsolescent. However, first this conclusion proved to be wrong, and secondly the underestimation of the entrepreneurial function in Walrasian economics was the result not of historical misjudgement but of its static nature in the sense indicated above. Lange's model illustrates the point well. He was concerned with the problem of solving the system of equations of general equilibrium, being aware that the CPB cannot know the technological coefficients which are to go into the equations, but assuming—in accordance with the neoclassical tradition—that the managers of enterprises and industries can obtain this knowledge provided they are given the prices of inputs and outputs. When the CPB provides them with these prices they begin the optimization procedure. However, optimization behaviour is only one of many aspects of entrepreneurial activity, and if there is concentration on this aspect only then the significance of choice among existing alternatives becomes grossly exaggerated, as if every single entrepreneur could know the complete list of available options. In reality the entrepreneur has to be an acute observer of the emergence of new alternatives, as well as a creator of them. His plans are based on expectations with regard to future developments, and as these take place in a world of continuous change in the relevant data, uncertainty is the inevitable framework and risk the unavoidable component of decision. The technological knowledge necessary to fill the elements of the Walrasian equations is not a datum but rather information which can only be discovered in the process of competitive struggle. Thus what matters is the peculiar entrepreneurial 'thinking technique', a kind of intuition, which is generated by actually finding oneself in a competitive situation. Such a situation exists in principle under capitalism, where entrepreneurs strive for profits, and this provides the foundation of the market coordination mechanism, which operates with huge imperfections but operates nonetheless.[12] As Kornai observes: 'In a genuine market process actors participate who want to make use, and can make use, of their specific knowledge and opportunities. They are rivals ... Some win and some lose. Victory brings rewards: survival, growth, more profit, more income. Defeat brings penalties: losses, less income, and in the ultimate case, exit!'[13]

All these aspects are absent in Lange's model of market socialism, which seems to corroborate the assertion that its claim to a convincing refutation of the Mises/Hayek challenge has been unjustified or at least exaggerated. Not only the problem of motivation discussed earlier, but also the problem of information which the model was explicitly meant to solve, remain far from being satisfactorily answered, despite the demonstration of the possibility of generating prices equally suitable for efficient allocation of given resources as those of the Walrasian model. Besides, the inclusion of the proper role of entrepreneurship and competition into the analysis shows that the two elements of motivation and information, usually treated as distinct though interconnected, are more like two sides of the same coin: the economic actor has to be appropriately motivated in order to engage in activity which generates the information necessary for efficient allocation in the broad sense, that is including the dynamic dimension. This of course raises in turn the major issue of socio-economic conditions: is such behaviour at all imaginable for economic actors who are not principals operating on their own risk and responsibility, but only agents employed by a public body which in itself is rather unfit for entrepreneurial behaviour? In other words, there recurs the problem of compatibility of market with socialism—the core of the Mises/Hayek challenge.

From an opposite point of view the same problem was posed by supporters of direct central planning as the dominant method of allocation of resources in a socialist economy. The simulated market within the sphere of production envisaged in Lange's model came under heavy criticism from these quarters as inconsistent with the proclaimed aim of continuous full employment, elimination of fluctuations, and equitable income distribution. The static characteristics of the model became the target, in the context of the likely conflict between the current equilibrium conditions and the need to effect rapid structural changes in productive capacities. On a more fundamental plane the concept of market socialism was criticized 'from the Left' as either bloodless capitalism without capitalists, of dubious efficiency and of even more dubious ability to meet socialist aspirations, or an opening through which genuine capitalism would force its way back.[14]

As we can see, the questions are numerous and serious. They do not, in our opinion, deprive the attempts to develop the theory of market socialism along the lines of Lange's model either of their place in the history of economic thought, or of their great importance for fostering change in the economic system of 'real socialism'. From the latter point of view the interwar debate certainly had the merit of advancing the idea of an alternative to the command system, as well as of showing how ill-founded was the traditional Marxist belief in the possibility of rational allocation of resources without prices reflecting scarcities. At the same time, however, it should be clear that when market-oriented reforms were put on the practical agenda in countries of 'real socialism' they had a strong foundation in the critical analysis of the deficiencies of the old system, but lacked an appropriate theoretical base for positive solutions. Lange himself admitted as much in his 1947 preface to the Polish edition (intended but abandoned for ideological reasons) of *On the Economic Theory of Socialism*, where he echoed an earlier private letter to Hayek in stressing the fundamental significance of the dynamic aspects omitted in the 'pure static solution given by me'; nevertheless, as the article 'The Computer and the Market' written shortly before his death seems to witness, he never succeeded in confronting the Austrian challenge as presented above.[15] Other contributions to the theory of market socialism made by Polish economists—and, as far as we know, by economists of other socialists countries as well—failed to do this either: those of non-Marxist provenance followed mainly the Walrasian approach, while Marxist pro-marketeers—including the present authors—formed the ranks of Kornai's 'naive reformers', viewing the prospect of the market–plan combination with excessive optimism. To some degree these theoretical failures might have been caused by politico-ideological constraints, but even in countries and periods when such constraints were at their lowest (for example, Poland 1956–7, and Czechoslovakia before the 1968 Soviet invasion), the full extent of the problems arising from the Mises/Hayek strictures was not brought into the open. It was only—or mainly, to be cautious—under the impact of the mostly frustrating experience of market-oriented reforms that the issues in question came to the forefront.

6

The Hungarian Practice

The first attempt to apply the ideas of market socialism to practical organization of the economy came in the early 1950s in Yugoslavia, after the Stalin–Tito break. The original motives of this change were perhaps not mainly economic, although the economic difficulties arising from the transplantation of the command system—initially the most complete in Eastern Europe and, paradoxically, voluntary—played a considerable part. The Yugoslav Communist Party searched first of all for political and ideological self-determination *vis-à-vis* the hitherto unquestioned authority of Stalin in the communist world. It was found in the concept of self-management, presented as an embodiment of that strain in Marxian ideas which emphasizes socialism as a social order which overcomes the alienation of labour by placing the means of production under the control of 'associated direct producers'. Self-managed economic units must be autonomous by definition, and consequently the command system had to be replaced by a system relying on market coordination. The change was envisaged as a continuous process culminating eventually in a fully fledged market socialism with limited and progressively weakening intervention by the state, which was destined to 'wither away'.[1]

As for the Soviet bloc countries, the dissatisfaction with the performance of the economy under the command system was the main motive for the reform drive. This dissatisfaction came into the open in the mid 1950s and quickly manifested itself in Poland (1956–7) in a relatively comprehensive blueprint of systemic changes aiming at a substantial increase in the role of the market. Similar ideas were widely discussed in Hungary, but the suppression of the uprising in November 1956 quelled attempts at economic reform. Interest in the idea of some combination of central planning with the market mechanism was shown in other countries as well, at the time also in China.

Since then, a long string of attempts at economic reforms—of various degrees of consistency, but heading in the same direction of increasing the role of the market—occurred in Eastern Europe:

Czechoslovakia in 1958; the New Economic System of the German Democratic Republic in 1963; the 1965 Kosygin reform in the USSR and its Bulgarian imitation; the economic component of the Prague Spring in 1968, suppressed with only slight delay after Soviet invasion; the Hungarian New Economic Mechanism introduced in January 1968; two minor Polish experiments in the 1960s (the second ending with the massacre of the workers on the Baltic coast in December 1970), and another—this time on a larger scale—in the mid 1970s. However, by the beginning of the 1980s out of all these attempts only the Hungarian New Economic Mechanism had survived; what happened otherwise were rather secondary modifications within the old framework of the command system.

The failure of most of the reform attempts was explained by the political resistance of the ruling elites; by the vested interests of the party and state bureaucracies, coupled with a reluctance on the part of the rank-and-file and the managers to trade security for stronger incentives linked to efficiency; and finally by substantive difficulties in devising and implementing a sufficiently consistent and workable reform project.[2] Fully acknowledging the part played by the two first groups of reasons, particularly the political one, we concentrate here on the substantive aspect, which is obviously of paramount importance for the entire subject of the book. This means we have to examine the two cases where the reformed system has actually been institutionalized: Yugoslavia, where the reform process was forty years old by the end of the 1980s; and Hungary, where the reformed system, called in 1968 the New Economic Mechanism (NEM), had by then passed the age of twenty. From the point of view of their longevity, both cases should provide sufficient material for some conclusions. The pertinent question, however, is whether or to what extent these conclusions will allow generalizations—and this is what we are looking for in the first place.

There are obvious difficulties in drawing general inferences from specific cases. Both Yugoslavia and Hungary are small countries compared with the USSR or China, and this factor alone must reduce the value of any extrapolation of their experience for a number of reasons, not least among them the very different degree of foreign trade dependence. Cultural factors deeply rooted in the past, geopolitical aspects, ethnic diversity or homogeneity—the list of points which make every case special can be long. Then comes the question of the criteria by which the success or failure of the reformed economic system ought to be judged in comparison with the past or with the non-reformed system. Overall performance—for instance, growth and/or welfare effects—must be taken into account, but this is fully meaningful only under the *ceteris paribus* clause; unfortunately that proviso is far removed from reality, which abounds in external shocks and a host of other influences over and above the systemic factor. As Granick said in connection with his analysis of the early results of the Hungarian NEM, 'Ideally, one would wish to evaluate the macroeconomic effects of the reform through a regression model which includes all important independent variables . . . and which treats the reform as a dummy variable'.[3] As long as this is not at hand, the elements of imprecision and impression in lieu of evidence will remain strong in attempts to correlate the systemic changes with macroeconomic performance. What seems to be easier in the light of available research results is to establish whether the economic reform has brought about the intended effects in the conditions of economic activity and the behavioural pattern of economic actors. In other words we want to know whether—and if so to what extent—the proclaimed graft of the market mechanism on to a socialist economy has resulted in genuine change in the way the economy operates compared with the traditional command system. The latter point is actually our main concern, although references to the macroeconomic effects cannot be avoided. It should be remembered, however, that our objective is not an evaluation of the systemic changes in the two countries in question as such (much more detailed analysis would be required for that purpose), but an examination of possible lessons for the marketization of socialism as a general proposition. After all, whatever the differences between individual communist countries, and even between Hungary on the one hand and Yugoslavia on the other, all have common fundamentals: ideological roots in Marxism-Leninism, a mono-party state; predominantly public ownership of the means of the production; and an extended period of operating the economy under a command system (except Yugoslavia). This does not make our exercise easier, but at least provides the ground for the attempt.

For several reasons Hungary looks the more convenient starting point: it is a case of a more 'natural' evolution of the economic system, unlike the *deus ex machina* origins of the Yugoslav reforms in the 1948 break with the USSR; it has produced a large critical literature by Hungarian economists themselves; and has unearthed problems which can be confronted later with Yugoslav attempts to solve them.

It is hardly necessary to go into the details of the 1968 economic reform in Hungary, which are rather well known.[4] Its major features can be described as follows. First, the proclaimed objective of the NEM was not that of a grand new design of socialism (as in the Yugoslav concept of self-management), or that of part of a wider idea of democratic transformation of the socio-political order (as could be detected in the course of the Prague Spring); the NEM was focused on increasing economic efficiency. Secondly, the provisions of the NEM, and even more the changes in practical policies, extended beyond the state sector of the economy, boosting cooperative organizations (genuine cooperatives, as distinct from the étatized cooperatives under the traditional Soviet system) as well as private economic activity. Thirdly, state enterprises formally ceased to operate on the principles of plan fulfilment (obligatory targets were abolished) and physical allocation of output and input (this was abolished too); they were to act as profit maximizers in free contractual relations between buyers and sellers, sensitive to prices and costs, exposed to the discipline of the market, and spurred to innovation and adjustment by the force of competition. These behavioural changes were expected to materialize despite the fact that the general proposition of the reform was not to renounce but, on the contrary, to improve central planning and render it more effective by removing the sources of the 'planning paradox' (see Chapter 4), by freeing the central organs from involvement in unnecessary detail, and by harmonizing national and local interests through the use of economic as opposed to administrative instruments. Crucial for the assessment of the reform as a whole is evidently the test of the validity of this proposition, which reflects the idea of combining planning with a (regulated) market. We shall concentrate therefore first on the state economy, leaving the discussion of the non-state sector to a later stage.

Let us begin with a bird's-eye view of the crude performance data, keeping in mind all the reservations indicated earlier. The national income (net material product) statistics[5] seem to indicate acceleration in Hungarian growth in the aftermath of the introduction of the NEM: the average annual rate of growth in real terms rose from 4.1 per cent in the 1961–5 quinquennium to 6.8 in 1966–70 and 6.3 in 1971–5, falling later to 3.2 in the 1976–80 period and to 1.4 in 1981–5. Kornai separates out the period immediately following the introduction of the NEM (1967–73), which shows an average annual rate of 6.1 per cent as against 5.7 for the preceding decade and 5.2 during the following quinquennium, with a steep fall afterwards; so the basic contours of the picture are similar.[6] Interesting, however, is that the periods of acceleration and slowdown of growth in Hungary correspond quite closely to the rest of Eastern Europe (apart from the USSR and Yugoslavia), which remained essentially unreformed; if anything the Hungarian slowdown was more pronounced, with 3.2 per cent of growth annually in 1976–80 against an average of 3.8 for Eastern Europe, and 1.4 in 1981–5 against 2.4 for Eastern Europe. Until the beginning of the 1980s the figures are decisively more favourable for post-reform Hungary with regard to agricultural production, in comparison both with the past and with the rest of Eastern Europe—but of course here we find ourselves largely outside the state sector. By all other conventional indicators—industrial production, fixed capital investment, dynamics of real incomes of the population, foreign trade and indebtedness—the story is more or less analogous to that told by the national income statistics. An important difference should be noted in the official consumer price index, much higher in Hungary than in other East European members of the CMEA (except Poland in the 1980s, of course), but this difference cannot be taken at its face value because of the change in the role of prices and the degree of equilibrium in the market for consumer goods and services. The quality of Hungarian statistical data— regarded generally as much better than in other East European countries—must also be taken into account.

Thus, without going into a more detailed analysis of the factors external to the operation of the economic system—such as demographic trends, which made Hungary worse off than almost any other East European country in increments to the workforce, or the particularly heavy losses in its terms of trade owing to the oil price shocks—one might say that the change in the economic mechanism heralded by the NEM did not produce tangible effects by the standard criteria of overall performance, either diachronically or synchronically. This statement must be immediately qualified, at the peril of being dismissed by every visitor to Hungary, particularly other East Europeans, well and justly aware of the wide range of favourable differences between that country and the rest of the communist bloc. The standard criteria of overall macroeconomic performance do not tell the full story: the post-1968 Hungarian economy is characterized by a much better equilibrated market than elsewhere in Eastern Europe, which makes monetary indicators more meaningful, as the dynamics of wages and prices reflected the dynamics of real flows more accurately, less distorted by endemic shortages. This is the result not only of acknowledgement by the policy-makers of the market-clearing function of price, and of the advisability in a trade-dependent economy like Hungary of bringing closer the domestic price structure to the relativities on the world market, but also of providing the state enterprises with greater room for manoeuvre as far as product mix and choice of inputs are concerned, and of enhancing the role of financial indicators. Under these circumstances a Hungarian state enterprise has become more sensitive to demand and costs than its counterpart geared under the command system overwhelmingly to plan fulfilment in physical terms; this could not remain without a positive influence on the quality and modernity of products, especially with regard to consumer goods where fashion is of significance. (Here again the direct and indirect impact of the wider scope for non-state activity ought to be kept in mind.)

However, all these necessary qualifications notwithstanding, it is indisputable that two decades of operation of the NEM (we stick to the designation of New Economic Mechanism, which has become a generic term despite its loss of novelty) have failed to produce the breakthrough which the reformers expected. Moreover, with the passage of time the benefits seem to wear off, as reflected in deteriorating performance towards the end of the 1980s, whereas the negative side-effects are being felt more acutely. The latter is particularly so in the social sphere, with stagnating and later falling average real incomes within the framework of widening differentials; the growing need to supplement the earnings from the 'first economy', which leads to the stretching of the working week to limits of endurance; the increasingly painful impact of inflation on some strata of the population; and so on.

Now comes the main question: has there been a qualitative change in the way the Hungarian economy operates under the NEM compared with the period of the command system? According to the overwhelming majority opinion of Hungarian economists, the answer is 'no'. This view is corroborated in a most clear manner by Janos Kornai,[7] who presents his own findings along with a comprehensive survey of Hungarian writings on the subject. Kornai distinguishes between two 'pure types' of coordination of activities and interactions of economic actors: bureaucratic and market coordination. Although in real life there is always some element of combination of the two, it is possible to distinguish between bureaucracy coordinated and market coordinated systems by assessing 'the relative strength of the components in the mixture'; hence, the modern capitalist economy can be classified as market coordinated despite some degree of 'bureaucratic intervention', and the Soviet-type command economy can be classified as bureaucracy coordinated despite the presence of some elements of the market. As for the post-1968 Hungarian economy, Kornai defines it as having undergone a change in the form but not in the essence of the coordinating syndrome; it has moved from direct bureaucratic control (by obligatory targets and physical allocation of resources) to indirect bureaucratic control (by using financial instruments to make enterprises comply with the priorities of the bureaucracy). In this context he puts forward the following proposition, which we quote in full:

The frequency and intensity of bureaucratic intervention into market processes have certain critical values. Once those critical values are exceeded, the market becomes emasculated and dominated by bureaucratic regulation. This is exactly the case in the Hungarian state-owned sector. The market is not dead. It does some coordinating work, but its influence is weak. The firm's manager watches the customer and the supplier with one eye and his superiors in the bureaucracy with the other eye. Practice teaches him that it is more important to keep the second eye wide open: managerial career, the firm's life and death, taxes, subsidies and credit, prices and wages, all financial 'regulators' affecting the firm's prosperity, depend more on the higher authorities than on market performance.[8]

The 'dual dependence' (on the bureaucracy and on the market, with the weight of the former predominant) manifests itself in a variety of ways in all aspects of the economic activity of state enterprises. They are to be the masters of their own output but have to conform to 'requests' from the ministries and other organs of economic administration, who regard themselves or are regarded as responsible for securing some predetermined level of supply to the domestic market or to export (in the latter case, state obligations in Comecon agreements play a particular role). They are given the right to choose their own input mix and suppliers, but have to take into account informal quotas and licences, which are sometimes even convenient in view of the still widespread symptoms of a seller's market in producer goods. They operate under a price regime substantially liberalized compared with the days of the old command system, but the degree of administrative regulation is still strong through direct fixing of some prices, detailed rules of cost calculations for prices supposedly left to the enterprise's own discretion, the obligation to report intended price changes in advance to the monitoring organs, and so on. They are free from an overall wage bill ceiling and its link with plan fulfilment, as well as from formal ceilings on employment, but again a number of restrictions are still applied in an informal way. It may be said that this list of bureaucratic (or administrative, in our own preferred terminology) regulatory devices illustrates merely the fact that old practices die hard, and that in spite of them both the room for enterprises' own decision-making has increased, and—more importantly—the criteria of evaluation and consequently incentives have shifted towards market-dependent ones like profitability, which after all determines under the NEM not only managerial and workers' bonuses or the amount of the development fund, but also the ability to pay basic wages and salaries. This may be true on the surface; the trouble, however, is that administrative regulation reaches deeply into the financial sphere by individualizing tax measures and subsidies, rationing credit according to criteria imposed from above instead of commercial considerations both current and prospective. In such a way, large-scale redistribution of funds from more to less successful sectors and enterprises occurs, which bails out the weaklings and restricts the high-flyers. Thus a greater emphasis on the financial aspects of performance may fail to offset the informal remnants of old command practices, and—paradoxically enough—strengthen the hand of the bureaucracy, which has the power to confer benefits on economic units if not whimsically then at least according to its own set of preferences. This not only makes the financial position more a function of the outcome of successful bargaining with higher authorities than one of market performance, as rightly pointed out by Kornai, but also carries in itself the threat of resurrection of the 'ratchet principle' in a modified form.

All in all, a Hungarian state enterprise finds itself under a 'soft budget constraint', that is it can count with a high degree of probability on being bailed out in the face of any bankruptcy threat, and—the other side of the same coin—it will not be barred from developing merely because it fails to meet commercial criteria, provided it is successful in the broadly defined bargaining process with bureaucracy. The power of the latter is particularly strong in the sphere of capital investment. The creation of enterprises' own financial base for investment (the development fund) not withstanding, the control of the main bulk of investment activity remains in the hands of the bureaucracy through direct budgetary allocations and the use of banking credit as an extended arm of the central plan. Last but not least is the bureaucratic control over managerial appointments, promotions, and demotions—obviously with strong political connotations.

The 'soft budget constraint' and the concomitant dependence of enterprises on administrative decisions affects adversely the potential of price relativities (including rates of exchange and rates of interest) to extract the desired adjustment in their behaviour. This in turn becomes an additional factor in seeking to effect such an adjustment through direct administrative pressure; hence there is less attention to the purging of distortions in the price structure, as well as less reliance on the force of competition in preference to direct intervention from above. (The very high degree of organizational concentration of Hungarian state industry at the time of introduction of the NEM is regarded by some observers as a reflection of the priority of administrative control over competitive conditions.)

Kornai illustrates the proposition that the NEM has not changed fundamentally the conditions of operation and consequently the behaviour of state-owned enterprises with a number of interesting accounts of empirical research. Examples include the shifts in the financial position of enterprises due to fiscal redistribution, and the characteristic differences in the structure of inventories between manufacturing industries in Hungary and those in some capitalist countries.[9] But the most striking evidence of this lack of change is provided by investigations into the question of the end-of-period phenomenon of 'storming', which is typical of the behaviour of enterprises judged by the criteria of fulfilling targets (formally or informally binding) for the period in question.[10] Contrary to expectations, Hungarian industrial enterprises display distinctive 'storming cycles', which may be taken as a convincing sign of their behaviour remaining largely similar to that of enterprises under a command system.

Several groups of reasons, by no means mutually exclusive, may be considered in an attempt to explain this state of affairs. The first is the failure to implement properly the provisions of the NEM. There is something to it, particularly in respect of certain restrictive measures introduced as 'transitory' (especially in the area of price controls) which have never actually been abrogated. However, the main complaints of distortion of the original blueprint relate to the period after 1972, when both topical and personal decisions of top party authorities unequivocally beat substantial retreat from the plan. The impression one gains from studying Hungarian writings on the subject is that the pre-1972 period is treated sometimes as a kind of 'golden era' of the NEM. And yet Granick's book,[11] based mainly on direct observations and interviews conducted in 1970–1, actually contains most of the assessments and conclusions which can be found, needless to say in a more elaborated form, in later Hungarian literature. Without the explicit use of Kornai's terminology, the conclusion that the Hungarian economy under the NEM still belongs to the category of those bureaucratically coordinated, albeit indirectly, appears in Granick's book as the categorical assertion of continuity between Romania, the GDR, and Hungary. In contrast,

> major discontinuity exists between the three CMEA countries on the one hand, and Yugoslavia on the other. The three CMEA countries share the common feature that each is guided by central planning and decision making from a single center. . . . While the methods of direction by the center differ substantially among the three countries, all are directed to the same goals: efficient execution of the center's decisions. . . . Instead, Yugoslav enterprises should be regarded to a considerable degree as independent power centers, whose actions are coordinated primarily through the market-place.[12]

Leaving aside the characterization of the position of Yugoslav enterprises, which we shall discuss later, the proposition that Hungary has remained in the family, as it were, even in the early period of the NEM is supported in the book by evidence similar to that mentioned above. Accepting the rather low degree of distortion of the blueprint in the initial practice of the NEM, the explanatory power of the misimplementation factor, although not without some value, can therefore hardly be decisive.

The second group of reasons is difficult to cover with one simple heading; perhaps the best would be the overriding policy objectives inimical to market coordination. Under this enigmatic formula many different things may hide, including the goal of preservation of the monopoly of political power by the ruling communist elite, or the goal of safeguarding the well-known and deeply entrenched vested interests of the bureaucracy (subjects which we have elected to omit in this book). However, under this heading we may also put noble, socially desirable policy objectives aiming at raising the level of welfare of the society, defined in a comprehensible and widely accepted way. This is the foundation of the concept used by Kornai in the last chapter of his *Economics of Shortage*—paternalism, which as a matter of principle props up a family member in difficulties.[13] Granick points in the same direction, but tries to be more specific by indicating as the main obstacle to market coordination the 'microeconomic full employment constraint' (life time job security in a given place of work), and less forcefully the 'price stability constraint'.

There is no doubt, in our opinion, that the pursuance of certain central policy objectives—whether of the noble or of the not-so-noble variety—may clash with the operation of the market mechanism, and that even allegedly selective overriding of market criteria may spark off a chain reaction, spreading administrative interference over a field much wider than the original source. Thus our second group of reasons is not to be dismissed. Once again, however, we think that it does not, by far, tell the whole story. Let us take, for instance, the 'price stability constraint'. It is quite plausible that it hampered market coordination in the initial phase of the NEM, but evidently less so since the late 1970s when substantial price movements began, with the official rate of inflation (consumer price index) reaching 7–8 per cent in the mid 1980s, and unofficial estimates putting it well into double digits. Nevertheless the relaxation of this constraint, as well as much greater flexibility in foreign exchange and interest rates, have apparently failed to enhance the role of the market mechanism relative to that of the bureaucracy. The case of the 'microeconomic full employment constraint' is more difficult to ascertain because it involves evaluation not of the facts themselves but of the motives behind them. It is true that a substantial reduction of the workforce in commercially unsuccessful state-owned enterprises has not been happening in Hungary, and that the use of the later enacted bankruptcy laws has been, at least until the end of the 1980s, an exceptional occurrence, more a publicity exercise than a working part of the economic mechanism. But to interpret these facts only (or mainly) as the effect of a deliberate pursuance of one particular kind of paternalistic objective, which is implied in the notion of the 'microeconomic full employment constraint', seems to us far-fetched. Unlike macroeconomic full employment, job security in a given place of work can hardly be regarded as an integral part of socialist ideology, including the official Marxist-Leninist doctrine. To our knowledge, the Hungarian leadership's policy statements during the NEM period (and before, for that matter) have not contained such a commitment; on the contrary, the calls for rationalization of the use of manpower have been progressively louder, with sincere attempts to apply concrete measures to this effect. If little has been achieved, the reasons might lie not so much in policy constraints as in the weaknesses of the economic mechanism, which has proved inadequate to elicit the desired responses. It may be of interest to recall in this context the characteristic Polish experience of 1982, when reform measures aimed precisely at shedding labour by state enterprises proved so ineffective that the early retirement schemes introduced in order to prevent macroeconomic unemployment resulted in widespread shortages of labour. As with every analogy, this example may not fully fit into the Hungarian situation, but it illustrates our point about the possibility of the system hindering rather than helping. This may be the case with some other manifestations of paternalism as well.

So, we are left with a third group of reasons for the failure of the Hungarian economy to cross the boundary between bureaucratic and market coordination: the inadequacy of the principles on which the system has been built, the faults of the reform blueprint itself. It may be argued that the distinction between the impact of the policy objectives inimical to market coordination and that of the blueprint of a market-orientated reform is not sharp enough to warrant a separate analysis. This has a grain of truth, but as our discussion of the Soviet-type development strategy and the command system has shown, the latter cannot be explained by the former alone. The same applies, in our opinion, to the reformed system: the new institutional solutions and their effects cannot be properly understood by simple reference to policy intentions. The Hungarian NEM, as well as a number of similar attempts at economic reform in communist countries, grew out of the same Marxist conceptual roots which saw the economic rationale for socialism in its capacity to operate directly according to the criteria of social costs and benefits, and not to limit itself to the private ones. The overriding role of central planning was to remain, the methods only were to be changed; hence arose the combination of macroeconomic planning with the market as the fundamental idea of the NEM. The postulated combination could of course be interpreted in many different ways, and it might not be viable at all. Whatever the conclusions, it seems clear that the conceptual framework of the NEM deserves not only to be treated separately, but also to be given special consideration. The Hungarian economic debates leave no doubts on this score, with the majority of the participants pointing out as the main flaw of the 1968 blueprint that it limited the operation of market forces, even in principle, only to product markets, while a market for factors of production, especially capital, has been barred.[14] Proper discussion of these problems requires *inter alia* a brief reappraisal of some aspects of the theoretical background of the Hungarian NEM.

7

Central Planning with Regulated Market—the Flawed Model

It should be stressed at the outset that whatever the strength of the negative position with regard to the market in general in orthodox Marxist theory, the attitude towards the capital market under socialism must be that of outright and uncompromising rejection. This is understandable enough, and obtains not merely on doctrinal grounds (the capital market, even limited to non-private participants, denies labour the alleged role of the ultimately single factor of production and the only legitimate non-exploitative source of income) but also because socialization of capital, its allocation on behalf and in the interests of the community as a whole, represents the mainstay of the postulated economic superiority of socialism over capitalism. The unfettered development of productive forces, the elimination of fluctuations, the removal of the absurdity of simultaneously having excess capital, excess labour, and unsatisfied needs—all this has been closely linked in Marxist theory with direct social responsibility for the accumulation and distribution of resources taken out of current consumption for the purpose of expanded reproduction. Hence there is no reliance on individual savings as a determinant of accumulation, and no place for the market in deciding how accumulation should be used, as Engels emphasized in reacting angrily to Dühring's idea of leaving the rate of saving to individual decisions: 'The most important progressive function of society, accumulation, is to be taken from society and put into the hands, placed at the arbitrary discretion, of individuals.'[1]

When the concept of 'market socialism' was expounded in the 1930s, Engels's stand that accumulation in a socialist economy must be a public concern was firmly upheld. Lange had no doubt that the rate of capital accumulation would be determined 'corporately', that is by the central planning board which would impose its own, and not the consumer's, valuation of the 'optimum time-shape of the income stream'. Lange calls this type of decision arbitrary and acknowledges the argument that it may involve diminution of the consumer's welfare, but the alternative—leaving all accumulation to the saving of individuals—'is scarcely compatible with the organization of a socialist society'. So the loss of the right to determine the rate of capital accumulation should be regarded as a price paid by the individual for living in a socialist society, the benefits of which richly exceed this particular cost; among the benefits he lists the overcoming of capitalism's inability to secure full utilization of resources, especially full employment.[2] A similar view is taken by Lerner as far as the collectivist (socialist) model is concerned, although his position becomes different with regard to the 'mixed but controlled economy'.[3] All this means among other things that an integral feature of a socialist economy must be an incomes policy on a macroscale, that is determination of the overall ratio of the aggregate value of incomes of the population (net of individual savings) to the total value of consumer goods and services in the given period (net of changes in stocks)—or, in simplified form, the relation of wages to prices and taxes. Thus elimination of the market from the sphere of determination of the rate of capital accumulation spills over in some sense to the labour market because it establishes limits beyond which no bargaining should move; perhaps it is this implicit link which prompted in the 1980s in Hungary the activation of the debate on the labour market simultaneously with that on the capital market.

The 'arbitrariness' of the determination of the overall rate of accumulation notwithstanding, Lange's model contains a capital market (or simulation of a capital market) for the purpose of allocation of investment between various sectors and projects: the allocating mechanism operates through the price of capital—the rate of interest—'simply determined by the condition that the demand for capital is equal to the amount available'.[4] However, as already mentioned in Chapter 5, the rationality of using this kind of mechanism for investment allocation met with sharp criticism by Dobb, who argued that the method proposed would either let in capitalist-type fluctuations or require very complex and cumbersome countercyclical measures.[5] Besides, both Dobb and other opponents of the idea of allocating investment through the market mechanism (for instance Paul Baran[6]) insisted on the superiority of direct central planning of investment through time, in view of the wider information available to the central planner compared with individual managers as to the future development trends of the economy as a whole, and the removal of the need to guess the future reactions of such managers to the (again guessed) future prices.

Scepticism with regard to the use of the rate of interest in a socialist economy was strengthened by the implications of Keynesian economics, and particularly by the firmness of Kalecki's statement that 'the rate of interest cannot be determined by the demand for and supply of new capital because investment "finances itself" regardless of the level of the rate of interest.'[7] At a later stage Kalecki was emphatic in maintaining that in a centrally planned economy the calculation of investment efficiency with the help of a surrogate rate of interest ('marginal recoupment period') can assist only in the choice of techniques for the achievement of given productive targets and the pattern of foreign trade, and not in the choice of the directions of change in the general structure of the economy.[8]

The theoretical argument against subjecting allocation of investment to the market mechanism fitted well with the concepts of economic reform gradually emerging in communist countries after the death of Stalin. The reformist Marxists were profoundly affected by the inefficiencies of the command system, but they—the present writers included—ascribed failures not to central planning as such but to excessive centralization, which clearly exceeded the capacity of the planners to collect and to process the flow of information. This seemed to be the result of the attempt to cover, by detailed obligatory target planning and physical allocation of resources, all aspects of current operations of state enterprises: size of output and its composition, labour and material inputs, sources of supply and directions of sales, prices, financial outcome, and so on. Decisions of this kind could and should therefore be left to the enterprises themselves, the horizontal relations of which would be coordinated by a regulated market. However, unlike current decisions, not only did the possibility of major investment decisions being taken rationally by the centre remain unquestioned; on the contrary, it was the market which was considered incapable of ensuring efficient allocation by long-term social criteria. Again, negative past experience in the field of investment was attributed to overburdening of the central plan with details of current operations, a defect which would be removed by leaving them to regulated market coordination. Needless to say, the ingrained ideology of socialist central planning and of socialist property relations, which were interpreted as giving to the state the exclusive right to create new productive capacities and determine the future structure of the economy, must have played a part in the tendency to limit the scope of change. The reformers (even those who were branded as 'revisionists') were prepared to move only some way from the old positions of the absoluteness of all-embracing planning. But, whatever the role of ideological (and political) factors, substantive considerations—the conviction that central choices between major economic alternatives can bring better results than the market mechanism— were, in our opinion, decisive for the virtual exclusion of the capital market from the reform blueprints which began to appear in communist countries from the mid 1950s onwards.[9]

A number of attempts to provide a theoretical foundation for the exclusion of the capital market were undertaken in the course of economic debates in connection with the search for an appropriate reform concept. Some of them, like that by the distinguished Chinese economist Sun Ye-fang,[10] based themselves on the Marxian distinction between simple and expanded reproduction as the guide on how to draw the line between the sphere of autonomous activity of an enterprise and that reserved for the centre. Some went beyond this distinction, arguing in favour of also giving to the enterprise the opportunity to expand and to modernize productive capacities, but still within its prescribed sector of activity, thus preserving the predominance of the vertical mechanism of redistribution of investment funds, and leaving the centre as the decisive force in determining both the rate of accumulation and the shape of structural change in the economy through sectoral and spatial allocation. To the latter category belongs also Brus's 'model of a planned economy with a built-in market mechanism', which is sometimes mentioned among the sources of inspiration for the actual Hungarian 1968 reform.[11]

One should never exaggerate the impact of a theoretical construct on practical solutions, especially in the case of systemic reform, which must usually contain elements of political compromise as well. Nevertheless, it can be said that by and large the blueprint of the Hungarian NEM followed the distinctions indicated above, albeit in the less rigid version. This comes out very clearly in an authoritative presentation of the main features of the reformed system published just after the introduction of the NEM.[12] Starting from the premise that 'the growth rates and major proportions characterizing the main processes of economic development can be best assessed and planned in the central planning organizations',[13] the role of the centre in allocation of investment was to be predominant. As I. Friss the editor of the publication, puts it:

In the new system a considerable and increasing part of investments will be realized on the grounds of autonomous enterprise decisions. In this field the state will assert its own points of view of investment policy mainly through the means of credit policy. But, in addition, the state has also other means of influencing decisively the main tendencies of development, namely by the centrally taken decisions regarding the largest investment projects, by the determination of a set of lump sums, each of which will be used for investments serving a special purpose, and, finally, by financing certain investments out of the state budget.[14]

Mention of bank credits in connection with enterprises' autonomous investment may suggest opening up an embryonic capital market (without using the term), but the qualification that 'also the credit policy of the banks is, in its main features, prescribed by the government and thus becomes another tool of planned economic control'[15] undermines this impression. Moreover, as an enterprise's own development fund (retained out of profits) is frequently insufficient for starting an investment, state directed bank credits become indispensable, which extends the planner's control even over the use of decentralized accumulation. This is one of the reasons why the statistical picture of the shares of central and decentralized investment activity in the Hungarian state sector does not reflect properly the respective scope of administrative coordination on the one hand, and market coordination on the other.

The renunciation of the capital market combined with the unequivocal interpretation of public property rights as exercised by the state administration was reflected in the NEM blueprint in the provisions concerning the foundation and liquidation of enterprises. The relevant quotation from Friss is rather lengthy but is instructive:

Evidently, *the considerable increase of enterprise autonomy* and the wider competence of enterprise executives *do not interfere with their dependence on the state as the owner of the enterprises* [original italics]. The autonomy is expressed, among others, in the right of disposition of the enterprises over their assets (within the limits set by legal rules) . . . On the other hand, their dependence on the state is reflected in the principles ruling that enterprises can be founded only by a minister or leader of a national authority or by the executive committee of a local council, and that the founder has the right to determine the sphere of activity of the enterprise, as well as to appoint and discharge its director and deputy director(s). Moreover, the founder may liquidate the enterprise if its activity is no longer needed by the national economy, if its profitable operations cannot be continued, or if the activity in question can be pursued more economically by another enterprise. Exceptionally, when national economic interests make it necessary, the founder may also order the reorganization of an enterprise. The founder may join several enterprises into a trust. . . . The founder has also the right and obligation critically to evaluate the activities of the enterprise as a whole and the work performed by the manager and his deputies, as well as to take decisions regarding their salaries and premiums.[16]

Quite consistent with this position is the shift of what may be called entrepreneurial risk connected with new technology to the economic administration:

'Economic and technical conceptions are elaborated for development tasks of differing scope and importance, at corresponding higher or lower levels of various organizations. Such conceptions must then be brought into relation between themselves and coordinated accordingly. Conceptions related to a branch of national economy must, in general, be elaborated by the competent ministry or another national authority; conceptions of national importance and those covering several branches belong to the competence of the National Board of Technical Development.[17]

What interests us mostly are the implications of the virtual exclusion of the capital market from the design of the NEM for those elements of market coordination which were supposed to operate and enhance the efficiency of the new system compared with the old. As in other matters, the separation of the impact of this particular factor alone is difficult, and one must be wary not to overstate its significance in relation to other factors likely to act in the same direction—to curtail the scope of market coordination in the economy. Nevertheless, we think—in the light of the Hungarian literature and our own analysis—that some valid links between the exclusion of the capital market and the weakening of the product market can be established.

The first, and obvious, corollary of the principles presented above is the need to retain a strong centre of economic administration ('bureaucratic coordination' in Kornai's terms). Any sort of economic dynamics requires a mechanism of intersectoral and spatial reallocation of resources for capital investment, and if the channels of horizontal reallocation are blocked, the function must be taken over by the centre which collects and redistributes funds through vertical channels. This might have been the straightforward intention in theoretical models like that of Brus mentioned above and in the blueprint of the NEM, but without apparently taking into account the inherent tendency of a body powerful in one field to spread its influence into other areas as well. The experience of all reform attempts in communist countries leaves no doubt as to the strength with which this tendency manifests itself in resurrecting the real control over supposedly decentralized economic activities by the central decision-makers. Furthermore, the blockage of horizontal flows of capital—except for the very minor role of the banks as genuine intermediaries, and not as 'another tool of planned economic control'[18]—creates a peculiar centralizing feedback. Enterprises deprived of the right to use their development fund outside the prescribed sphere of activity tend to invest as much as possible internally, which may lead to inefficient allocation; in order to prevent this, higher administrative organs, having a wider purview of opportunities, react with restrictions on freedom of enterprise decisions.

The second implication of the elimination of the capital market concerns the role of the centre in the distribution of national income. A macroeconomic incomes policy which allows effective adjustment of the overall ratios of investment and consumption in the broad sense is an indispensable element of a planned economy in pursuance of the objectives of avoiding demand-determined fluctuations and of securing full employment and a high level of capacity utilization. This, as indicated earlier, requires control over prices and wages; however, in the absence of the capital market, which would in part allow the trade-off between current and future benefits to be influenced also by enterprises and even households (as lenders), the full burden of such control falls on the shoulders of the centre. Inevitably it becomes more rigid and more detailed, as witnessed for instance by the most elaborate scheme for the division of enterprise profits between the sharing and the development funds in the very design of the NEM. The same has been true of the rules of wage regulation, particularly after the initial general ones (control of average wage with punitive taxation in case of excess) have proved inadequate and have been subjected to rather frequent changes as well as differentiation by industries; needless to say, the degree of arbitrariness and the dependence of enterprises' wage policy on their administrative superiors must have increased. All this must bear on the operation of the labour market (see below).

Competition is the third issue to be discussed in connection with the attempt to use the market mechanism without a capital market. The negative experience of the command system has taught the reformers that competition has its benefits, and, both in theoretical model-building and in most of the blueprints of the new system of functioning of the economy, the role of competition has been linked to the rejection of the Stalinist claim that excess demand under socialism spurs production; market-clearing prices have been firmly postulated as an indispensable means to overcome endemic shortages, as well as a generator of signals for adjustment in product mix and input composition. Short of proposing abolition of controls over foreign economic relations, the familiar form of 'state monopoly of foreign trade' with its 'price equalization mechanism' isolating the domestic from the foreign market, has been expected to give way, at least gradually, to interaction between the two markets via 'trans-action prices' (prices paid or received in foreign markets converted into domestic prices by a single exchange rate) modified by a normal system of tariffs and duties; this should create a competitive alternative both for the producers and for the consumers.

Expectations with regard to this external impetus to competition proved overoptimistic for reasons of balance of payments constraints, which in turn reflected a combination of external shocks and the insufficient adaptability of the economy. This apart, however, the good intentions of promoting competitive behaviour generally have not been properly tested, either in theoretical writings or in the reform blueprints, against other, sometimes fundamental, features of the aimed-at reformed socialist edifice. To begin with, this has been the case in respect of one of the main planks of the claim to socialism's superior economic rationality—the capacity to employ fully human and material resources. How does this affect the conditions, the scope, and the directions of competitive behaviour? The answers to this questions have been rather vague—ranging from acceptance of the need for 'some' excess supply (including 'some' unemployment) to the insistence that aggregate correspondence between demand and supply at full employment level can never mean partial equilibria everywhere, hence the room and incentives for competition. The reference to unavoidable partial disequilibria is certainly correct, but if the capital market is excluded there is no reason to expect competition for a place in the developing sectors because the boundaries between sectors cannot be crossed on enterprises' own investment initiative; at most, competition may emerge within the limited framework of shifts in the markets for goods that it is possible to produce on existing assembly lines. Even less likely under the circumstances must be the kind of competition generated by the entrepreneurial spirit of 'creative destruction',[19] the essence of which consists not of adjustment leading to restoration of equilibrium but of disturbance to the existing equilibrium by the opening up of new opportunities; without access to venture capital and new spheres of activity there is no room for such processes. This in itself does not yet mean that disequilibria cannot be countered and new opportunities sought; however, this must take place not through the mechanism of competition but through appropriate administrative regulation, which is a different proposition, regardless of how the comparative efficiency of the two allocation mechanisms may be evaluated. As for combating monopolistic behaviour, the obvious requirement is that of free entry into sectors and areas involved, which is clearly connected with the possibility of horizontal flows of capital. Theoretically, as in Lange's model, free entry can be simulated by an appropriate rule; in practice, it is again the centre which may act accordingly, treating the maintenance of competitive conditions as one of the criteria of capital allocation, the establishment of new enterprises, and so on. However, the likelihood of the latter course of action is small because it runs counter to the interests of effective central control (a small number of larger units is easier to control than a large number of small ones), not to mention the exaggerated perceptions of economies of scale which are characteristic of economic bureaucrats. All in all, the idea of having competition in product markets or within the sphere of current economic decisions (in terms of Brus's model), without opening up some sort of capital market, has hardly been proved.

Finally, the fourth element of the implications of the bar on the capital market in the design of the NEM and its theoretical antecedents is the impact on the disciplining function of the market, or—to revert to Kornai's widely accepted terminology—on the hardness of the budget constraint for state enterprises. This is connected but not identical with the problem of competition discussed above; after all, one can have strict financial and other norms imposed on subunits inside a larger organization without putting them into mutually competitive relations, as practised for instance in quite a number of multidivisional capitalist corporations. It is in the subjection of state enterprises to the discipline of the market, which would enforce the heeding of the correct signals on what and how to produce, that the main contribution of the economic reform has been expected. The essence of the concept of central planning with a regulated market mechanism has been to make the enterprises profit-oriented through the appropriate incentive scheme and to confront them with 'parameters of choice' (that is with monetary magnitudes, or prices in a general sense) independent of their volition and applied in uniform way to all. These parameters were to reflect the macroeconomic priorities of the central plan and to translate them into binding guides for action on the microlevel; they could include subsidies in cases of special preferences, but fixed in advance and product-specific, not differentiated by enterprises and following their balance sheet. And yet, as pointed out in the previous chapter, the 'parametric system' of managing the economy has failed to materialize properly in Hungary where, to use Granick's formulation, 'financial tutelage was substituted for the earlier physical planning.'[20] This failure is linked particularly strongly to the lack of capital market by several Hungarian economists, especially so by Tardos.[21]

As far as investment activity is concerned, the 'softening' of the budget constraint becomes an unintended effect of the high degree of concentration of decisions in the hands of administrative authorities, particularly at the centre. This means, on the one hand, that investment demand of enterprises is not constrained by the test of the market-place, and their success in obtaining funds depends on their ability to convince the bureaucracy of the relevance of the project. The problem here is thus that of information—the capacity of the centre to assess independently the project in question and to compare it with the range of alternatives available. On the other hand, contrary to the implicit or even explicit assumptions of the model that the centre is a homogeneous representation of societal interest, in reality it may more often than not seek a compromise between various partial interests, and hence become susceptible to pressure. The problem here is that of motivation—the capacity of the centre to withstand particularisms for the well-perceived sake of the whole. Taking into account that under the circumstances the centre is almost the only barrier to investment demand, the likely inadequacy of its information and motivation structures must have highly damaging effects not only for macroeconomic equilibrium, but also—in the context of our discussion—for the financial discipline of enterprises. A frequent secondary consequence appears as well: when completed defective projects are put on stream they give rise to *sui generis* legitimate claims for support from the administration, and so become a source of breaks in financial discipline of current operations as well.

However, the implications of the lack of a capital market for softening the budget constraint in current operations are not limited to the aspect just mentioned. The most serious implications, as emphasized by Hungarian economists, consist of engendering conditions which make it extremely difficult, if not outright impossible, to expose underperforming enterprises to the threat of forced curtailment of their activities, and ultimately of bankruptcy. If a currently unsuccessful enterprise is prevented from attempting to raise capital in the market in order to restructure its operations, including branching out into other more promising fields, or cannot be taken over by a more dynamic firm which sees latent opportunities, strict application of the market rules of the game would actually lead to gross inefficiencies: not only would those enterprises unable to recover go out of business, but also those with good prospects although in temporary difficulties. Under the circumstances, in the absence of the evaluating mechanism of the capital market, the administration must step in—which again opens the gates to arbitrary breaks of financial discipline. Tardos summarizes this side of the experience of the NEM in the following way:

At present the New Economic Mechanism is unable to apply financial pressure successfully as an adjustment method not only because without central interventions the generally introduced rules would push an unduly large number of enterprises into bankruptcy, but also because, in a market system, bankruptcies infer the existence of free capitals ready to take over the ruined enterprises. Such free capitals are lacking [in Hungary] as a consequence not of capital scarcity, but of the centralization of incomes and of the fact that, if at all, only so much is left with the enterprises as necessary for the economic objectives agreed with the centre. Thus the government could not allow a general hardening of the financial constraint. During the last almost twenty years the central organs have been continuously forced to use not only the methods of intervention declared to be normative . . . but also openly differentiated interventions of varying intensity, and different for each enterprise . . . Central organs often approved increases in producers' prices and were compelled to grant individual tax exceptions, subsidies and preferential credits.[22]

This amounts to an unequivocal proposition that the roots of the softness of the budget constraint for economic units cannot be reduced to paternalistic policies in general and to the principle of microeconomic job security in particular, but should be traced to flaws in the design of the system; even explicit abandonment of such policies would not be sufficiently effective against the inherent systemic tendencies.

On the whole the case for the capital market seems strong in the light of the Hungarian experience, which has revealed the inconsistencies of reform concepts limiting 'the regulated market mechanism' to produce markets alone. Another question—too early to take up at this stage of our discussion—is the scope and shape of the capital market, its relationship to the economic role of the state, and in particular its viability in the framework of socialist ownership.

Less clear, as far as we can judge, is the criticism frequently voiced in the Hungarian economic literature as to the lack of provision for a labour market in the design of the NEM. One should expect a labour market actually emerging whenever there is freedom of choice of occupation and place of work—in other words when people are not assigned to jobs by order of the authority. In so far as the practice of administrative and penal (forced labour in the strict sense) assignments diminishes, we can speak of a labour market even under a command system. Admittedly, within the dominant state sector this is a most peculiar market, with a single general employer who himself establishes the rules which cannot be openly challenged (the bar to the challenge is very much a consequence of the political system). Nonetheless, relative prices of labour (wage differentials) have to be used in the process of allocation, and the necessity to adjust wages (and/or other forms of remuneration) to the changing conditions of supply an demand has to be recognized in one way or another, quite often in breach of the regulations from above. The switch from the command system to the NEM has undoubtedly broadened the sphere of operation of the labour market and enhanced the autonomy of enterprises, which are less constricted by obligatory targets and the physical distribution of producer goods, and in particular are under the influence of increased activity outside the state sector. Of course, taking into account what has been said above about the true overall relationship between administrative and market coordination under the NEM, the labour market must also have failed to come up to expectations, especially as certain traditional provisions for the protection of employees' rights (for instance, the legal obligation of the management to present specific personal reasons for every dismissal) continued to affect labour mobility.

However, behind the ill-defined demands to 'introduce' a labour market in the new stage of economic reform in Hungary seems to lie a real major problem: how to create conditions which would allow the fundamentals of the process of wage determination to be brought out of the administrative sphere into that of market coordination. We have stressed several times already the importance of income distribution (the price/wage relationship) for macropolicy objectives, as well as the link between the lack of capital market and the scope of state regulation in this field. But there is more to it: the absence of market-type opposition of interests between 'buyers' and 'sellers' as far as labour is concerned presents a formidable obstacle to the achievement of a market ('rational') price of labour, and by itself throws the door open to bureaucratic coordination. The managers of state enterprises are not intrinsically motivated to limit wage payments; they will try to do so under outside pressure only, and if there is not (or insufficient) 'budget constraint' generated by the market then this means pressure from above, that is of an administrative nature. Hence arises the perennial struggle in all reform attempts to find a replacement for wage control in the command system, the main instrument of which is the linkage between the *planned* wage bill and *planned* output (corrected for over- or underfulfilment by a normative coefficient again fixed from above). Since the introduction of the NEM in 1968 several methods have been tried with very mixed success, and with the rather plain message that the more effective the control the less efficient becomes the allocation of labour by market criteria.

Therefore, if the criticism of the lack of a labour market is meant to imply that both the managers and the workforce in state enterprises should be subject to the discipline and allocative mechanism of the market, then it is valid (which, of course, is not the same as to say that it can provide easy solutions). To some extent the activation of the labour market depends on the consistency of operation of other elements of the market mechanism, as well as on more resolute macroeconomic policies. But in many respects it depends on the possibility of regenerating a true bargaining process, and this in turn—needless to say—touches upon fundamental aspects of the essence of socialism.

To sum up: flaws in the very concept of 'central planning with regulated market mechanism' which underlie the design of the NEM have to be regarded as not the only but evidently a serious and perhaps even the main substantive reason for the failure to subject the Hungarian state economy to market coordination. The elimination of the capital market from the blueprint is apparently to be blamed in the first place for the fact that the role of market-type institutions within the state sector has been reduced mostly to that of a new form of bureaucratic coordination. Instead of interacting with the plan on a macroscale, market-type institutions have been used by and large as instruments of the plan, different from the previous command ones, but ultimately serving similar purposes and producing roughly similar effects. The experience of the NEM in this respect has shown that even such an important measure as the abolition of obligatory output targets and of rationing of producer goods, which for a long time has been hard fought for (in most countries unsuccessfully) by the reformers, can fail in bringing about a major change in substance when necessary complementary factors are missing. The significance of this lesson in the need to distinguish between form and substance ought not to be overlooked in assessing other aspects of the reform process in countries of 'real socialism' as well. This is by no means tantamount to saying that a limited reform of the NEM-type was immaterial, and therefore those who opposed it in the past were to be absolved. Despite its limitations, such a reform should be regarded as a first substantive step in the right direction, preparing further changes, and making them easier.

The demands, followed by tentative practical steps, to institute a capital market as well as to widen the labour market—in Hungary, in China, in Poland, even in the USSR at the end of the 1980s—reflected to some extent conclusions similar to those presented here. However, by this time some experience of attempts to abolish administrative wage controls and to introduce certain forms of capital market (without the name!) into a socialist economy was already at hand—the Yugoslav experience. Consequently, we turn to the examination of the record of the Yugoslav reforms.

8

The Yugoslav Lessons

As far as the Yugoslav experience is concerned, our main interest is in the reforms of the first half of the 1960s. These were introduced with the clear intention of crossing the watershed between an economic mechanism combining administrative with market instruments, in many ways similar to the Hungarian NEM (but with a strongly accentuated self-management component), and a fully fledged 'labour-managed market ecomomy'.[1] These reforms—we use the plural because some measures started in 1961, with the major change coming in 1965—were presented as further steps on the road to 'self-management socialism' a grand design challenging the Soviet-type étatist model.[2] At the same time, however, the reforms were expected to produce pragmatic gains, providing conditions propitious for economic efficiency, allegedly hampered by the insufficient consistency of the previous systemic framework. (In the course of the fervent debates in the mid 1980s yet another—slightly cynical—reason was put forward, namely that because of the impossibility of the constituent national republics agreeing on the priorities of federal investment policies, an acceptable solution could only be found in decentralization of decisions.)

Two major issues which have come up in our discussion of the Hungarian NEM were confronted in one way or another in the Yugoslav reforms of the 1960s. First, in 1961 enterprises were given the right to determine autonomously the division of their net income (value added after taxation and social insurance payments) into personal incomes and retained funds. Previously this division was rather tightly controlled both by the trade unions (from the point of view of wage relativities) and by the local authorities (communes) who were interested in determining the level of investment activity. Simultaneously the role of the banks was enhanced and the foreign trade regime liberalized.

Secondly, in 1965 the quantitative dimensions of the distributional authority of enterprises were raised through the reduction of the tax burden and the reduction, followed later by abolition, of interest payments on the capital assets with which they had been endowed by the state: the share of enterprises in gross value added rose from 47 per cent on average in 1960–3 to 59 per cent on average in 1967–71.[3] Concomitantly the 'social investment funds', which had been the main instruments of mobilization and allocation of investment resources by the state, were abolished, and their unexpended balance was transferred to the banks, which also accumulated loanable funds for investment credits. The main direct federal state investment responsibility which remained was the fund for the accelerated development of the underdeveloped regions. As a result, a substantial shift occurred in the proportions of investment funds under different institutional control: The share of 'social funds and budgets' (that is federal, republican, and local government) fell from 60 per cent in 1960–63 to 20 per cent in 1972, that of the banks (private savings excluded) leapt from 3 to 42 per cent, and that of enterprises ('basic organizations of associated labour' (BOAL), as enterprises or their autonomous parts became known after 1976) changed only marginally from 37 to 38 per cent. The lack of correspondence between the increased share of enterprises in total value added and the almost stable share in investment funds was thought to be caused by the working collectives' preference for higher personal incomes over investment.[4]

Neither of these important groups of changes has been presented in the Yugoslav economic literature of the time as an introduction or broadening of the labour market or of the capital market respectively.

The concept of the labour market is hard to reconcile ideologically with the idea of socialism in general and self-management socialism in particular; the latter is supposed to associate workers and not to hire them, hiring being perceived as the maintenance of the sale–purchase relationship between the owners of labour power and the owners of the means of production. Soon after the launch of self-management, wages were replaced by personal incomes, which are supposed not merely to have symbolic meaning but to reflect the new reality of labour also sharing the entrepreneurial function and hence being entitled to the residual above costs and external obligations. Practice simply could not follow the full logic of this conceptual transformation, both because of cost calculations and because of the need to determine in advance the basic portion of the workers' income. Hence there appeared guaranteed income levels differentiated by branches, in addition to the 'minimum personal income'— a flat sum established by law, equal for all types of work, and paid out as the ultimate safeguard of an employee's subsistence. But regardless of fine points of theory and their relation to practice, it is clear that the freedom obtained by enterprises in the distribution of income has enhanced the capacity to adjust their wage ('personal income') policies to the conditions of supply of and demand for labour. In this sense the reform contributed to the development of a labour market, although with many peculiar features stemming from the general institutional framework of the Yugoslav economy.

The capital market is also not among the most popular of notions in the Yugoslav ideological terminology, despite the fact that at least since 1961 some forms of money market have been in existence, and that even in the 1950s part of state investment funds have been auctioned among enterprises on the basis of the rate of interest they offered.[5] But whatever the terminology the reforms of the 1960s, especially that of 1965, were meant to open the allocation of investment resources to the market mechanism. The fundamental element of the move in this direction was to be the shift of responsibility for expanded reproduction, as the Marxian term goes, from the state to enterprises, or—according to the widespread Yugoslav formula— from the political to the economic sphere. More scope for the self-financing of investment activity was provided to enterprises; and, as the division of net income into accumulation and personal incomes was left to their discretion, enterprises were to choose between present and future gains through the assessment of market parameters. Interenterprise, intersectoral, and interregional redistribution of investment resources was to proceed mainly not by the vertical route through the state budget (except for the special development fund mentioned) but horizontally: through direct investment in or lending to other enterprises, and through the banking system. As seen from the figures above, the banks were to become the paramount vehicle of financial intermediation. They were to operate on commercial principles within the framework of the government's monetary and credit macropolicy, the targets of which were supposed to switch 'from qualitative objectives focusing on the sectoral allocation of investment to quantitative objectives focusing on its overall level'.[6] Under such provisions the banking system could be regarded as an element of a capital market, particularly if measures were taken to avert the threat of the banks' excessive power. These comprised the rather substantial scope for self-financing, supplemented by the pooling of enterprises' resources, bond issues, and so on, as well as an organizational structure for the banking sector in which enterprises were to be in a strong position. In accordance with the Banking and Credit Act of 1965, commercial ('basic') banks—unrestricted in their operations to a given zone of activity—were to be established by enterprises and state organs ('socio-political communities' at the local, republican, or federal level) as equal partners contributing to the bank's own capital (credit fund) and becoming shareholders. The bank management was to be controlled by the founder members in proportion to their share in capital, subject to a maximum of 10 per cent of votes to inhibit monopolization. The changes in the investment and banking system had been accompanied by the proclamation of wide-ranging deregulation of prices and further streamlining of the liberalized regime in foreign economic relations.

Under close scrutiny, the afore-mentioned measures would require numerous qualifications and careful separation of the formal from the substantive. Nevertheless most Yugoslav economists would concur with the previously cited characterization of post-1965 Yugoslavia as a 'labour-managed market economy'. Perhaps some disagreement would surface with regard to the completion date of its later transformation into a 'contractual' (dogovorni) economy, but this is less relevant for our problem. Similarly, many outside analysts have no doubts on this score: for instance Granick, on the basis of investigating Slovenia in 1970, felt justified in quoting the Yugoslav economist Bajt to the effect that 'the Yugoslav economy is run along Adam Smith lines to a degree which is quite unusual for Europe as a whole';[7] and ten years later Lydall concluded that 'Yugoslavia shares with capitalism one very important characteristic, namely, a market economy.'[8] Thus, at least for the aftermath of the reform of the early 1960s and at least in certain respects, there is good reason to examine the Yugoslav experience from the point of view of the claimed inadequacies of the concept of the Hungarian NEM discussed in the preceding chapter.

Let us begin again with a look a the performance of the economy, keeping in mind—as in the case of Hungary—all the necessary reservations.

The evaluation of Yugoslav economic performance in particular periods is generally more difficult than for most other countries of 'real socialism' because of strong short-term fluctuations, which make the outcome very much dependent on the time spans chosen for comparison. Probably the best suited for our purpose is the comparative analysis conducted by Jože Mencinger,[9] who arranges his data

Yugoslavia: average annual rates of change for key economic
indicators (per cent, in constant 1972 prices), and supplementary
efficiency ratios

	1952–62	1963–73	1974–84
Economic indicators: rates of change			
Gross domestic product	8.3	6.5	3.9
Industrial output	12.2	8.6	5.4
Agricultural output	9.2	3.1	2.1
Employment (except agricultural)	6.8	2.4	3.6
Export (current $US)	12.0	14.0	13.3
Import (current $US)	10.1	16.6	11.8
Investment in fixed capital	11.5	5.3	1.0
Private consumption	6.5	6.4	2.8
Retail prices	3.6	13.0	28.3
Efficiency ratios			
Investment/GDP ratio	41.99	38.87	35.21
Capital/output ratio	2.28	2.23	2.64
Employment/output ratio*	3.87	2.42	1.86
Share of unemployed in workforce	5.01	7.58	13.29
Share of value of imported goods covered by export	64.66	69.44	63.96

* Number of employed in the social sector per 1 m dinars value of output in 1972 prices.

according to three successive 'economic systems': the 'mixed administrative and self-managed market economy' 1953–62, the 'labour-
managed market economy' 1963–73, and the 'contractual economy'
since 1974 with data up to 1984. (In view of the obvious problems
with the precise pinpointing of a system transition, Mencinger chose
to take the promulgation of a new constitution as the beginning of
each period.) He gives the average annual rates for the key economic
indicators shown in the accompanying table. (We omit the data for
the period of 'administrative socialism' 1946–52, and the special data
for 1980–4.) These rates are supplemented in the table by a number
of ratios which may be taken as tentative indicators of comparative
efficiency, despite the lack of clarification as to the methodology of
their computation.

The picture which emerges from these comparisons is striking:
unlike the Hungarian first post-reform period (see Chapter 6), which
brought an improvement perhaps not pronounced but nevertheless

discernible, the Yugoslav post-reform period shows, with few exceptions, a marked deterioration in economic performance. The preceding system, which we regard as in many respects analogous to the
Hungarian NEM, clearly comes out on top, and it is of little surprise
that one of the participants in the heated debates of the mid 1980s
has described it as the 'golden period' of Yugoslav economic development.[10] Of course, a number of special factors contributed to the
'gilding' of the period in question. First, US aid totalled $2 billion
during 1949–61, which was very substantial by the standards of the
time, amounting to 28 per cent of the value of imports.[11] Secondly,
there was the 'reserve of past mistakes', as Kalecki has described the
once-and-for-all effect of the elimination of the gross absurdities of
the administrative hyper-industrialization drive (this has been particularly evident in agriculture, where the 9.2 per cent average annual
growth of output in 1952–62 has succeeded the average annual *fall* of
3.1 per cent in the years 1946–52). Thirdly, some projects delayed
from the preceding period could be put on stream with lower current
investment outlays. Fourthly, a more general decelerating trend
might have set in at a higher stage of development, although this is
strongly denied by some Yugoslav economists.[12]

Despite the possible influence of especially favourable circumstances on the 1952–62 record, and certain positive signs under the
'labour-managed market economy' (faster growth of labour productivity in the first place, and also an improvement in the balance of
payments towards the end of the 1960s), the overall results of the
reforms must be judged as greatly disappointing, not only from
strictly economic but also from social and ethnic-national points of
view. Deceleration of growth accompanied by accelerated price
inflation and rising unemployment, which could not be curbed even
though the frontiers were opened for massive migration to Western
Europe, bred popular dissatisfaction, particularly among the workers.
The combination of the shift of economic power away from federal to
republican and regional government with the greater role of market
forces seems to have favoured the more highly developed parts of the
country, thus exacerbating national conflicts. The first open political
reflection of increasing tensions came in 1968 with the threat of
workers' support for the Belgrade student protest; this was followed
by the nationalist outbreak in Croatia in 1970–1, dangerous not only
in itself but also because of its implications elsewhere. The perception
of the link between the negative economic results and the political
tremors is said to have become sufficiently strong to persuade the

ruling elite of the need to divert from the clear-cut market-socialist road. The new 1974 Constitution, and particularly the Associated Labour Act (Zakon of Udruženom Radu or ZUR) of 1976, plus the Planning Act of the same year, are treated today rather unanimously as an actual substitution of 'self-management social planning' for the market as the main coordinating mechanism. 'Self-management social planning' is supposed to be compatible with the market, as it is meant to operate through voluntary agreements between self-management entities and through contracts with and between state authorities on various levels. In practice, however, the new system ushered the country into a veritable maze of bureaucratic arbitrariness in which the local organs of the single ruling party (the League of Communists of Yugoslavia) wield the greatest power. The ensuing economic mechanism not only failed to provide any kind of effective coordination ('neither market nor plan'), but also greatly contributed to the further fragmentation of the national economy into a loose federation of six republics plus two autonomous regions, with the republican (regional) authorities well placed to intervene comprehensively in the allocation of resources. Dubbed 'polycentric étatism' by a number of Yugoslav economists, the 'contractual system' is regarded as the major cause of the relentless slide of the country after 1976 into the full-blown economic and socio-political crisis of the 1980s.

However fascinating the examination of the validity of the above assertion might be, it is not this problem which ought to concern us here, but the reasons for the apparent failure to benefit from and to sustain the market-socialist stage. On this issue the opinion of Yugoslav economists seems to be pretty strongly differentiated. We shall try to present briefly the main currents of opinion—not an easy task in view of the complexity of the matter and shifts in the dividing lines on particular questions.

One current of opinion points to the concept itself as the reason for the failure of the attempt at fully fledged market socialism. In a book which can be regarded as representative of this view, K. Mihailoviĉ maintains that the reforms in the mid 1960s actually upset the emerging 'equilibrium between the plan and the market, initiative and coordination, requirements of macro and micro economics'.[13] By shifting the responsibility for expanded reproduction to enterprises they moved from the one-sidedness of the early postwar administrative system, which excluded the market from the production sphere altogether, to another one-sidedness of excluding the plan altogether. The market was called upon to fulfil functions beyond its capability, at least in a socialist economy: to determine the shares of accumulation and consumption in national income, and to determine the sectoral and territorial structure of investment. The capital market is particularly unsuitable for these functions in a less developed economy which suffers from shortage of capital. Overloading the market in this and other respects inevitably leads to the necessity for corrective administrative intervention, which however cannot restore the lost systemic equilibrium and results in the 'neither market nor plan' chaos. Under the special Yugoslav circumstances, planning at the federal level becomes the main victim of the attempt at excessive marketization, which makes the administrative backlash most effective at the level of the republics and autonomous regions, with all the ensuing bad consequences of fragmentation of the economy. It is interesting to note that Mihailoviĉ does not mention at all the Hungarian criticism of the operation of the NEM and the possible implications for the validity of the model of the planned economy with a built-in regulated market mechanism, which he himself seems to favour in substance.

The opposite current of opinion maintains that not the concept of market socialism but rather timidity and incorrect implementation have been responsible for the disappointments and ultimately for the changeover to the ill-conceived 'contractual' system. Not everybody holding this view seems to have been prepared to endorse without qualification the bluntness of Bajt, who states simply that 'the lack of success of the 1965 reform is predominantly the effect of insufficiently large dose of the market.'[14] However, judging from the comprehensive discussion of 'all our economic reforms'[15] in 1986, the degree of consensus with regard to the failure of the market in general and of the capital market in particular to operate properly has been very high. Among the most characteristic qualifications voiced in the debate has been the criticism of the effective elimination of all forms of macroeconomic policies, which left the operation of the market completely without control, free not so much for competition as for monopolitic preying. The proponents of this type of criticism have not spelled out the kind of policies (or planning) thought indispensable, but presumably what has been implied in the first place was the lack of coherent national fiscal and monetary policy (a phenomenon emphasized in the World Bank reports as well), and not the kind of central planning advocated by the Mihailoviĉ current of opinion. Among the weakest points of the implementation of the reforms brought out in the debate was the lack of attention to the pricing of production factors (as distinct from product pricing), and especially to the price of capital. Not only were enterprises freed of the charge on their endowment capital, but also the rate of interest on bank credits was kept well below the rate of inflation. Very probably this bizarre policy might be traced to the institutional setup of the banking system. The banks could hardly remain independent and commercially minded against the powers and interests of their controlling shareholders, the 'socio-political communities' and large enterprises, both of whom were interested not so much in the banks' profits as in the cheapness and the softness of loans. With liquidity provided in various forms by the weak National Bank, the negative consequences for the operation of the market were manifold: enterprises—particularly those in stronger positions vis-à-vis the banks—could pay out higher personal incomes at the expense of internal accumulation (sometimes even of depreciation as well) and apply for investment credits, the excess demand for which could not be matched by an appropriate increase in the rate of interest. As a result, allocation of capital by the price mechanism had to be replaced by non-price rationing, which brought the controlling state organs even more into the decision-making process, enabling them to influence the physical structure of investment, and in particular to prevent the interregional mobility of capital. The inflationary effect of this mechanism is evident, the more so that—contrary to the impression of a buyers' market in comparison with other communist countries—the 'soft budget constraint' was a familiar phenomenon in Yugoslavia, enterprises being allowed to default on debts and payments for deliveries, or simply being bailed out by local administration. To what extent this laxity was motivated by social considerations is difficult to ascertain, but it is worth mentioning that one of the participants of the 1986 reform debate suggested that 10 per cent of enterprises (with over half a million employees) would have to be closed down if strict financial criteria were applied.[16] It is also interesting to note that a number of Yugoslav economists emphasize the failure to develop competitive conditions domestically through liberalization of external economic relations.

If one accepts the line of argument of this second current of opinion—and to us it seems on the whole plausible—one would have to say that, despite appearances, even in the heyday of the 'labour-managed market economy' Yugoslavia presents a case of an abortive attempt at introducing a limited capital market (as well as a labour market in the sense discussed earlier) rather than a case of deteriorating performance as a consequence of institutionalization of such a market. This does not invalidate entirely the first diagnosis (as distinct from the therapy) of the harmful effects of dismantling the old system of investment allocation before putting in its place a better one. And from the latter point of view—to be able to put into operation a better allocative mechanism—the Yugoslav experience with the 1963–5 reforms, as Laura Tyson rightly says, 'suggests some of the difficulties that a switch from a traditional plan system of capital allocation to a market system is likely to encounter'.[17]

We do not intend to go here into the examination of the reasons for these difficulties in the Yugoslav case as such. The political factor clearly plays a very substantial part, strongly emphasized in the public discussion on economic reforms, although often without the necessary degree of concretion. Another obvious culprit is the ethnic national problem of enormous complexity, which for many years was rather pushed under the carpet instead of being examined for viable compromise solutions. There are, however, two groups of issues which have to be looked at in the Yugoslav context in view of their significance for some general aspects of market-oriented economic reforms in countries of 'real socialism': the position of the private sector; and, even more important, the economic effects of self-management.

As for the first, Yugoslavia—unlike Hungary (and China, or Poland after 1987)—has benefited little from the interaction between reform in the state ('social') sector and the enlargement of the scope of the private sector. The experience of the Hungarian NEM has shown that the latter not only responds quickly to market stimuli with increased supply of goods and services, particularly vital during the transition from one system to another, but also exerts competitive pressure on some areas of the state sector itself, thus becoming a *sui generis* catalyst of the reform process. This happened very little in Yugoslavia in the course of the reforms of the 1960s, not because the share of the private (and small cooperative) sector was low by comparison with other communist countries, but because the reforms failed to lift the numerous restrictions which hampered its potential to exert greater influence on the market. For instance, by 1980 over 90 per cent of the active workforce in agriculture was employed privately, but mostly in subsistence farming on poor land, badly equipped, and without the possibility of area concentration (a statutory maximum of 10 hectares of arable land had been in force since the early days of the communist regime). The low relative incomes of private farmers and the lack of prospects were among the powerful factors behind the massive process of migration to towns, which not only exacerbated the unemployment problem but also left private agriculture increasingly in the hands of elderly, poorly educated people, with a high proportion of women in charge. As for the non-agricultural private sector, formal restriction on employment (Lydall [18] gives a figure of five non-family workers as a maximum) was continuously accompanied by administrative harassment and fiscal pressure, the least perhaps in tourism and catering, which attracted foreign currency investment out of remittances and money brought back by workers returning from abroad. Needless to say, formal restrictions were evaded on a large scale and moonlighting became a widespread practice, but this—though exerting a substantial influence on income distribution—did not have the positive effect on the overall operation of the economy which could be observed in Hungary, or China, as a result of legitimization of some areas of private and genuine cooperative activity in the course of economic reform. Within Yugoslavia itself there are many who attribute the higher degree of marketization and the relative efficiency advantage of Slovenia *inter alia* to the contribution of private and cooperative enterprises, which enjoy greater legitimacy than in most other parts of the country.

As far as self-management is concerned, its implications for the functioning of the economy have been for a long time the subject of a theoretical debate and attempts to find empirical evidence in support of the various positions. The main issue in this debate, started in 1958 by Ward,[19] has been the behaviour of a self-management enterprise in comparison with a capitalist one operating under analogous market parameters. In particular, the question has been whether the former would *ceteris paribus* reach its optimum with lower output, lower employment and higher capital intensity than the latter, because the objective function of a self-management enterprise is maximization of income per worker and not of profit. There is no point in surveying this debate here; the interested reader may turn to some of the publications referred to in note 19. What is worth noting, however, is that in the search for possible ways to overcome the crisis, the debate flared up again in Yugoslavia itself, and that this time those who were rejecting outright the Ward type of argument found themselves strongly challenged.[20]

Our direct concern is the implication of the Yugoslav form of self-management for the capital and the labour markets. A Yugoslav enterprise is not a cooperative in the usual sense of capital being collectively owned by the members, with each member retaining a stake in the total value of assets, as well as the right to withdraw and to dispose of it subject to adopted rules. The capital of a Yugoslav self-managed enterprise—both the initial part handed over in the past or currently to newly established enterprises (since 1965 free of interest), and the part accumulated out of the retained net income—is said to be owned by the society. The workforce of the enterprise (or, strictly speaking, of the 'basic organization of associated labour') can be described as a sort of trustee body in charge of managing social assets, fully entitled to usufruct, and hence also responsible for entrepreneurial risk. However, all these rights and responsibilities related to an individual worker are based exclusively on employment, and are irrevocably lost with its cessation. This gave rise to a hypothesis, advanced first by Furubotn and Pejovič,[21] that workers in a Yugoslav enterprise, acting rationally from the point of view of their self-interest, would be less inclined to reinvest the residual collectively than to distribute it as personal income, which—if privately saved—would create assets at the individual's own disposal. The figures mentioned earlier, showing the stagnating (later even diminishing) share of enterprises' own funds in total investment finance, has been taken as empirical corroboration of the above hypothesis. This is disputed by some Yugoslav economists, [22] who claim that the phenomenon in question results simply from the wrong policy of negative real interest rates, which makes the distributional behaviour of the self-managing collective perfectly rational. But as we have pointed out in describing the organization of the banking system, the interest rate policy itself may be linked with the low propensity of self-managed enterprises to reinvest their own funds. In any case, taking into account the difficulty in apportioning the specific weights of various factors in practical developments, one can say that the empirical evidence is at least logically consistent with the hypothesis. Thus, in so far as the self-management system undermines the certainty that future returns will accrue to those who take the present investment decision, and opens up the possibility that somebody else will enjoy the benefits of accumulated assets, the basis for the capital market is weakened.

A similar conclusion seems plausible with regard to the scope for horizontal mobility of capital through direct investment outside the existing enterprise—either by investing in another enterprise, or by creating separate production units as subsidiaries. In the first case, the only avenue open is some kind of merger, which often means sharing returns regardless of the relative strengths of the partners; acquisition of a capital stake with a concomitant place on a management board, let alone a fully fledged takeover, goes of course against the grain of the system. In the second case, the possibility of a subsidiary breaking away and becoming an independent self-managed entity must be taken into account, particularly when the new unit is located in another region, with likely support from local authorities; this means transformation of the original capital outlay into a simple loan, which is an entirely different proposition. Moreover, division of larger enterprises into autonomous BOALs may even create obstacles to intra-enterprise capital mobility, and in so far as such fragmentation is being justified by the need to keep the size of the unit down for the sake of real workers' participation, this ought to be regarded not as an aberration of policy but as one of the corollaries of self-management. The limitations to horizontal capital mobility affect adversely the reality of the principle of 'freedom of entry' into other sectors or areas; in a situation when the potential for redistribution of capital on a national scale is reduced to a minimum, and the local governments display strong autarkic tendencies, this becomes quite conducive for creating monopolistic positions.

As for the implications of self-management for the labour market, the first observation is that the rules of the system do not leave room for wage bargaining. Formally there are no sides which could bargain, either because of conflicting interests (capital owners versus wage earners) or because one side (such as the state) takes upon itself the representation of wider and longer-term interests against current particularisms. In so far as a self-management collective is free to decide how to distribute net income (as approximated in Yugoslavia immediately after the regulations of the early 1960s) it is in a position similar to that of a self-employer, who himself has to strike a proper balance between the present and the future, taking into account the pressures and prospects of the market-place. However, the similarity ends when the property rights aspect is considered, as well as factors which soften in reality the budget constraint of the self-managed enterprise. All this creates great obstacles to the operation of a labour market. In practice a barrier must be erected to contain the tide of wage pressure; in Yugoslavia this has often been done by informal administrative intervention, or—in emergency situations—by a formal wage freeze. Whatever the method of administrative intervention, its frequent use is in itself a sign of labour market failures.

Of course, market conditions have an influence on the general capacity to pay out personal incomes by Yugoslav enterprises in so far as they have to adhere to the 'principle of distribution according to the market-verified results of work'[23] or—in simple terms—in so far as they are limited by their total net revenue. This, however, raises a new problem: income differentials and the market. Income differentials for the same type of work between enterprises and branches due to variations in performance are judged to be not only higher than either in capitalist or in other countries of 'real socialism' but also much more persistent because of the obstacles to mobility of factors of production connected with the self-management system. The link with low mobility of capital was noticed above. As for labour, the issue most often underlined in the Yugoslav economic literature is the unwillingness of the more successful collectives to dilute their gains by taking on additional labour either from the ranks of the unemployed or from other enterprises and regions—an assertion consistent both with the observed tendency to relatively capital-intensive investment and with the particular difficulties in fighting unemployment.[24] Again, this does not mean that determination of the level of personal incomes in a given enterprise can be completely divorced from the position elsewhere, and that no mechanism operates toward equalization of remuneration of the same kind of work. But as pointed out by Popov,[25] under self-management conditions this mechanism displays peculiar asymmetry: a strong tendency to match any average increase in the branch as a whole, but a very weak or non-existent tendency in the opposite case. This upward flexibility and downward rigidity of personal incomes must be another factor aggravating inflation and unemployment.

This discussion has not been intended, and should not be taken, as an attempt to assess the validity of the self-management idea in general, either in the purely economic or in the socio-political aspect. It has been aimed exclusively at the implications of self-management for the prospects of developing capital and labour markets in a socialist economy. The conclusion that self-management of the Yugoslav kind blocks such prospects entirely would perhaps be too strong, but that it adds substantially to the difficulties seems correct. However, probably the most important lesson from this experience, as well as from the indisputable differences in responsiveness to the NEM by the state and non-state sectors in Hungary, is the necessity to examine the question of links between the operation of the market and the type of capital ownership. This will be done in Part IV, preceded by an analysis of the macroeconomic implications of fully fledged market socialism.

PART IV

Market Socialism—the Problems Ahead

9

The Capital Market and the Problem of Full Employment

Our discussion of the experience of market-oriented economic reforms in some countries of 'real socialism', as well as of normative theories underlying these reforms, has shown that the half-way house of a product market alone, especially without a capital market, has failed to bring about the desired change from bureaucratic to market regulation and hence to provide the answer to the problems of inefficiency plaguing socialist economies. This view is shared by many economists both outside and inside the communist bloc, and has already become a kind of conventional wisdom. In abstract terms, it does not necessarily follow from such an assessment that the only way out of the inconsistent position is to press further ahead with the market. Coherence may also point in an opposite direction—to comprehensive planning, perhaps with better organization of the economy and more sophisticated techniques. But the overwhelming mood in countries of 'real socialism', especially with the Chinese reform drive and the Soviet *perestroika*, seems to favour a market-based consistency. We are not here going to argue for or against one alternative or another. But as the market tendency seems to be prevailing and more likely to be pursued in practice in the foreseeable future, we intend to explore the problems which such direction of development of 'real socialism' may bring about.

We shall call *market socialism proper* (MS) a consistently reformed system, which although still based on state ownership in one form or another includes a capital market along with the product and labour markets. As it is clear that the main innovation of MS compared with the half-way houses consists of the introduction of the capital market, we shall concentrate on this question.

THE CAPITAL MARKET—THE NEEDS, FORMS, AND EXPECTATIONS

It seems appropriate to begin with a brief restatement of the argument in favour of the capital market in the context of market-oriented reform. The direct source of inefficiency and thus of a shortage economy under both the *command system* (centralistically planned economy or CPE) and the *regulated market system* is the persistence of the soft budget constraint, to use Kornai's terminology. Why is there this persistence? Our tentative answer goes along the following lines. A hard budget constraint means full dependence of the performance of the enterprise (firm) on its own revenue. But if an enterprise is to be judged exclusively on its financial results it must have the right to use all the available opportunities to survive and develop. This involves investment decisions, including those pertaining to product and process innovation both inside and outside the firm, as well as inside and outside the branch if the intrafirm and intrabranch opportunities are limited. Besides, the adherence to the principle of free entry related to this possibility is indispensable if competition is to be taken seriously. Indeed free entry, actual or only potential, is a necessary condition of competitive pressure. Thus the decentralization of investment decisions seems to be part and parcel of the systematic change aiming at hardening the budget constraint of the enterprise. At the same time, decentralization of investment decisions opens the way to entrepreneurship and to innovations, which are mostly connected not with current decisions, but with investment. In turn, decentralization of investment decisions generates the need for a capital market. Otherwise the surplus in the hands of the enterprise, increased as a result of the reduction of the state's revenue accumulated hitherto for central investment, could be invested only within the enterprise itself, either for expansion of the existing production lines or for creation of fully owned subsidiaries; the size of the firm's investment would at the same time be constrained entirely by its own savings. This would be a very cumbersome and highly restrictive system, curbing the reallocation of resources to a greater extent than the old redistribution mechanism through the central budget. Even the proper handling of the depreciation fund would present problems under these circumstances because of the possible asymmetry in time between accumulation of the depreciation fund and its reinvestment.

In the most general and simplest sense a capital market provides the mechanism of horizontal reallocation of savings through transactions between the savers and the investors in productive assets (entrepreneurs). We do not need here to go into the intricacies of this mechanism, which in practice involves a labyrinth of intermediate stages and diversions. It is enough for our purposes to concentrate on the ultimate functions of the capital market in an economy with a decentralized investment process. What may, however, have some implications for our further discussion is the distinction between major forms of the capital market: direct credit relations between firms, commercial banking, the bond market, and the equity market (the economic literature quite often reserves the very term 'capital market' for the latter two).

As far as direct credit relations between firms are concerned, long-term capital lending is rather a rare occurrence in contemporary Western market economies, and there is no reason to believe that it would be different under MS. Developed credit relations in the capital sphere require clearly specialized institutions of financial intermediation. This function is widely performed in the market economies by the commercial banking system. The need to create such a system has been recognized in all countries of 'real socialism' which started the process of decentralization of investment; by the end of the 1980s incipient forms of commercial banking appeared in Yugoslavia, China, Hungary, Poland, and the USSR. The creation of state commercial banks was tantamount (at least formally) to dismantling of the traditional mono-bank system in which the functions of the central bank (CB) were merged with that of a single accounting, clearing, and crediting institution of a virtually administrative nature. The change involved a number of technical problems (like, for instance, the method of providing the commercial banks with their initial statutory capital), but the main issue was of course the real 'commercialization' of the commercial banks, that is their true separation from the state administration and their freedom to act as profit-pursuing enterprises.

Keeping in mind the inevitable learning process as well as other factors, the experience to date can hardly provide sufficient clues to the actual part that commercial banks can play in the capital market under MS. Our assessment must therefore be mainly hypothetical. Nevertheless it seems correct to say that the banks may to a large measure satisfy the needs deriving from decentralization of investment, even disregarding other possible forms of the capital market. In some developed capitalist countries (Germany, Japan) the banking system played for a long time an evidently greater role in the process of capital allocation than the securities market, and it might well be that this could repeat itself in MS evolving from 'real socialism'. Banks are obviously not simple intermediaries beween savers and business borrowers, but active creators of credit money by being able to lend out a multiplicity of the deposits attracted. Performing this function, they can and do vary the quantity of money, thus influencing the rate of interest and allowing the level of investment to vary. The banks' ability to expand or contract the amount of investment credit on commercial grounds would contribute to the hardening of the budget constraint for the investors. As at the same time, the structure of the network of commercial banking is typified usually by the leading role of a comparatively small number of large banks, the CB would gain a relatively effective instrument of monetary policy. The task and the substantive potential of monetary policy will be discussed in the third section of this chapter.

Despite the rather considerable scope for the banks' activity in this area, it should hardly be expected that they could remain the only element of the capital market in MS. This opinion is based not so much on the fact that in some countries of 'real socialism' (China, Hungary) the emergence of a bond market actually preceded the establishment of commercial banking,[1] as on a number of features which banks cannot contribute but the market in securities can. One of such factors, common to both the bond and the shares market, is the introduction of flexibility in the repayment date of a loan by the opening up of a secondary market (or through a buyback procedure). A secondary market attenuates to some extent the conflict between the desire to borrow long and the willingness to lend short. The market for securities, particularly with a secondary market, increases the risk element for the saver (the spectre of capital loss) but at the same time provides the prospect of capital gains. On the whole this may extend the size of the capital market by attracting more and concentrating otherwise dispersed savings, and in addition may encourage speculation, which speeds up the movement of capital, while making it less predictable.

Particularly high expectations are associated by the radical reformers in countries of 'real socialism' with the market in equity shares.[2] The main reason is the belief in the strong efficiency-enforcing impact of the market's assessment of the enterprise's (joint stock company's) performance, culminating in the role of takeovers (including the pressure of potential takeover bids) and the closely linked process of continuous valuation of capital on the stock exchange. Among the factors more specific to the problems of transformation of 'real' into market socialism, emphasis is laid on the greater chance of making a state enterprise truly independent from the state administration by turning it into a joint stock company, which might admit explicit representation of various interests on the board of directors, or even introduce a mixed-economy element inside the enterprise by allowing minority holdings of individuals and/or cooperatives. Share owner-ship by employees is expected to raise the degree of involvement of the workforce in the overall performance and to combine it with a level of responsibility unattainable in an ordinary self-management setting devoid of an individual capital stake.

Needless to say, the expectations associated with establishing a capital market in a socialist economy are often unduly inflated. No market operates with textbook smoothness, even when the picture is drawn under assumptions of imperfect competition. This is especially the case with financial markets, whose movements reflect in the Western world many influences which have nothing to do with the real business of production and exchange. The hope that a socialist economy would perform the miracle of both having the cake and eating it, of reaping the possible benefits of the capital market without paying the price, if it still lingers is obviously ill founded. To the contrary: it is by no means certain that the need for decentralization of investment and the intertwined need for the capital market, as presented at the outset of this section, is feasible at all in a socialist economy defined as a system in which public (state) enterprises dominate. The capability of a public enterprise to operate under a hard budget constraint in conditions of uncertainty has yet to be examined (Chapter 10). However, for the moment assuming the feasibility problem is solved, the question of the macroeconomic consequences of the introduction of the capital market must be faced.

The sections which follow constitute an attempt to discuss these consequences along with possible means of dealing with them. Needless to say, most of this discussion will have to be conducted in theoretical terms, leaving unexplored the many problems of how to build bridges between theoretical abstractions and the complexities of socio-economic practice. Even in terms of a pure theoretical model we disregard many important problems. Thus we assume that the economy consists of state-owned firms only; hence the question of the relation between state and private ownership of the means of produc-tion is not being analysed. The most important simplification is, however, that of a closed economy. We deal, rather shortly, with the complications caused by the relaxation of this assumption at the end of this chapter.

FLUCTUATIONS AND UNEMPLOYMENT IN MARKET SOCIALISM

It is very difficult to analyse a system which does not yet exist. It should, however, not be impossible to envisage some of its regularities if it has to share certain common features with the capitalist system whose experience has been investigated for a long time. Of course there is no generally accepted theory of a capitalist system, but a few hypotheses are commonly accepted, at least by particular schools of economic thought. Bearing this in mind it may be advisable to declare that the present writers share the fundamental elements of the Keynes-Kalecki approach to problems of economic dynamics; the analysis which follows will use this approach.

The feature which MS shares with capitalism is the position of the enterprise (firm). The firm in MS has to be motivated exclusively by short- and long-run profits, as well as by an increase in the value of its assets. It has to be financially fully responsible for its activities and to act in a competitive environment which requires *inter alia* a free entry and exit arrangement. The only—but important—difference (at this stage of the analysis) is the exclusion of private ownership of the means of production. Thus the firm is expected to behave exactly as its capitalist counterpart. If the firm is a joint stock company, it is assumed that the socialist manager is as efficient and caring as the capitalist one, although on the board of directors he faces only the representatives of the state or of other state firms and institutions as shareholders. It is assumed, too, that the board's decisions are governed by profitability considerations only. These are, of course, very strong assumptions on which our results depend. Our task here is a tentative investigation of how such a system can be expected to behave in terms of macroeconomic stability and growth.

MS means a truly monetarized economy in which all goods (and not only consumer goods, as in a CPE) are supplied as commodities. They are produced for sale, and only after they are transformed into money (that is, into generalized purchasing power) is the production process complete. The transformation of commodities into money (their realization, in Marx's parlance) constitutes the critical phase in the reproduction process of a monetarized economy. Indeed, the realization of commodities under these circumstances is not automatically assured. On the one hand, savings mean withdrawal of purchasing power from circulation, and thus supply without corresponding demand. On the other hand, investment means injections of purchasing power into circulation, and thus demand without corresponding supply. Under these circumstances the realization problem cannot be solved without taking into consideration the relation between savings and investment.

Let us imagine that the whole economy is being divided into two vertically integrated sectors producing investment goods I (sector 1) and consumer goods C (sector 2). The value added of each sector is distributed between wages W and (gross) profits P, where profits include all factor payments other than wages, as well as depreciation. Wages are spent on consumption without any time lag, while profits are saved.

Let us start with sector 2. Given the price/cost ratio, the value of the output C divides into two parts, corresponding to the wage bill W_2 and to the profits (or the surplus) P_2 of sector 2. The first part is being sold to the workers of sector 2; the second, however, cannot find a market inside this sector. If, and only if, investment goods are produced in sector 1, resulting in a wage bill W_1, a market for the surplus would arise. If $W_1 = P_2$ then the demand for consumer goods would correspond to their supply. If we add P_1 to both sides of this equation we get $W_1 + P_1 = P_1 + P_2$; that is, $I = S$, where S denotes (gross) savings equal to investment.

The equality between investment and savings must hold *ex post* under all circumstances. However, which factor is active and which passive? Intended investment follows investment decisions with some time lag; hence it is exogenous in a given short period. Savings in the same period are, or are mainly, an increasing function of (gross) national income Y, that is $S = S(Y)$; hence savings constitute an endogenous variable. If we disregard unintended changes in inventories, Y has to reach a level at which $S(Y) = I$, this level being called equilibrium national income Y_E. Thus every level of investment, (below a certain level discussed further) determines, given the savings function, a level of national income which is adjusted to the size of the market. In that sense total demand creates its own supply, contrary to Say's Law. However, the equilibrium national income may or may not reach its full employment level Y_F depending on the size of investment. If savings are a proportional function of national income with a rate of savings equal to s, then $I_F = sY_F$, where I_F denotes the full employment level of investment. With $I < I_F$ we have $Y_E < Y_F$; the smaller is I in relation to I_F, the greater is unemployment.

Before we proceed further we have to make some assumptions concerning prices and costs. Prices can be divided into two groups— those determined by demand and those by cost.[3] To the first group belong raw materials and agricultural goods, whose supply is inelastic in the short run. When demand increases (decreases) so do prices, the quantity remaining unchanged. To the second group belong all other goods. Their supply is, within limits, elastic. When demand increases (decreases) so do quantities, while prices remain proportional to costs. If costs do not change then prices do not change either.

We shall deal in this chapter with cost-determined prices only and disregard demand-determined prices. We will assume that average, variable costs are constant and begin to increase only when full utilization of capacities is approaching. As far as the price/cost ratio is concerned we shall assume that it is determined by the degree of imperfection of the market and remains constant (or at least sticky, that is changes only slowly) before capacity bottlenecks become effective. With the price/cost ratio remaining constant (gross) profits increase *pari passu* with output; hence the savings rate (equal to the share of profits in national income) remains constant too.

Let us now assume that (real) investment following some previous decisions increases by dI and the wage bill in sector one by dW_1. If there is unemployment (which allows for the increase of investment in the first place) the output of sector 2 increases until the surplus increases by dP_2 equal to dW_1. The increase in the output of sector 2 is dC and must be bigger than dP_2 because the wage bill in sector 2 also increases, by dW_2. Taken together, national income $Y = I + C$ increases by $dY = dI + dC$. The well-known relation dY/dI is called the investment multiplier and is greater than 1. Analogous considerations apply to the case of $dI < 0$. Thus any change in investment results in a multiple change in national income and in a change in savings equal to the change in investment. Indeed, from $dW_1 = dP_2$, by adding to both sides dP_1 we get $dW_1 + dP_1 = dP_2 + dP_1$ and $dI = dP$ or $dI = dS$, because an increase in profits means an equal increase in savings. Hence investment is the active and saving the passive factor, and the medium through which investment creates saving is the volume of national income.

We have considered up to now a pure quantity adjustment which implies the existence of unemployment (and of free capacities) and a constant price/cost ratio (not necessarily constant prices). Now we move to a discussion of a situation in which full employment exists already. Then the mechanism described can no longer function. Indeed, with full employment, investment can increase only to the detriment of consumption because a shift of labour between both sectors has to take place. Given the level of the money wage rate, the wage bill W_1 must increase, while the surplus P_2, given the prices, must decrease; this results in the demand for consumer goods exceeding their supply. If the prices of consumer goods increase in relation to wages, equilibrium on the consumer goods market can be regained but the price/cost ratio would change. Instead of a quantity adjustment as described earlier we have now a pure price adjustment process. The volume of the national income does not change while its structure is being changed.[4]

A pure price adjustment is not very likely in a market economy in which investment decisions are ruled by profitability considerations only. Indeed, the whole process has started by an assumed shift of employment from sector 2 to sector 1. This shift need not succeed, however, because sector 2 would try to keep its workers by offering higher wages when sector 1 tries to outbid them. If the shift of labour does not succeed, the initial increase in money wages would be passed to prices without further consequences. If some shift has initially succeeded it will come to an end rather soon. Indeed, prices must increase faster than money wages, and an inflationary development is to be expected as workers would defend their real wages. It is hard to imagine that the workers would accept a lower real wage with an increased nominal demand for labour. On the other hand, the increase in costs would inflate the prices of investment goods and, possibly, negatively affect the investment expansion which has put into motion the whole process in the first place. We shall assume in our further analysis that, before full employment is attained, quantity adjustment prevails with the price/cost ratio constant (or sticky).

The capitalist economy is characterized by both a relatively constant price/cost ratio and investment fluctuation; the investment fluctuates because expectations concerning its future profitability fluctuate too. As a result, national income and employment in a capitalist economy fluctuate together with investment. Kalecki has seen in the constancy of the price/cost ratio in capitalism one of its main weaknesses. The expected flexibility of this ratio in a socialist economy was judged by him as its very advantage.[5] However, he had in mind a socialist economy in which some central authority (let us call it by the traditional name of central planning board or CPB) would fix both investment and prices in relation to money wages, that is costs. The practice of the CPE has in general supported his view; that is, if investment happens to be reduced (in relation to national income) the CPB would reduce the price/cost* ratio, thus preventing the decline in national income and unemployment.[6]

In this sense the CPE is not a demand-determined but a supply-determined system. The volume of the national income is determined by the existing capacity and labour force (including the level of efficiency characteristic for this system); it is, however, independent of the level of investment. MS is intended to be a demand-determined system. It should, therefore, be expected that under the impact of market forces the old price 'inflexibility' would reappear. In other words, the distribution parameters would recover their primary role and the changes in national income would follow the changes in investment activities. The problem to be analysed under these conditions is the expected investment behaviour of firms in MS, assuming that only firms are entitled to make investment decisions. These decisions are not repetitive; they have long-run and mostly irrevocable consequences; and, which is most important, they involve risk because of uncertainty related to future events. Thus expectations concerning the future will play an important role in investment decisions.

The expectations of firms will depend crucially on the hardness of the budget constraint. The harder the budget constraint, the deeper the conviction that the very survival and growth of the firm depends uniquely on its profitability, the more the expected profitability would influence investment decisions. But is is not only investments that involve risk: lost opportunities may become equally dangerous if more aggressive firms prevail over the timid ones in real, rivalrous competition.[7] Thus an important element of expected future events is the presumed activities undertaken by other actors in the economic environment, which in turn depend on their own expectations concerning the future. Under these circumstances the firm will try to guess what are the expectations of other firms, and the latter will do the same. This interplay of expectations will result in investment decisions whose final outcome is quite hard to predict.[8]

In practice the investment decisions of a firm will be influenced by market signals, which can—and must be—interpreted as a proxy for the state of expectations, which otherwise cannot be observed. Another important factor is the financial situation of the firm. It will be determined by the firm's own capital and by its liquidity as well as by access to the capital market, that is by the credit possibilities open to the firm. Own and borrowed money will determine the maximal level of investment the firm is financially able to undertake.

Whether the firm would use more or less fully these financial possibilities depends upon concrete investment projects and expectations about future returns and costs. Product and process innovations promising new markets and/or new cost reductions would stimulate investment decisions. The same role will be played by the level of and changes in profits. Indeed, given the capital stock of the firm these factors determine the rate of profit and its changes. It is impossible to formulate an investment decisions function in MS; formulation of such a function is a stumbling-block in macroeconomic analysis even of existing systems. It seems more useful to concentrate on the most important features which can be expected, judging from the experience of capitalist market economies, to manifest themselves in MS. These features are the cumulative tendency of investment decisions and their instability, which are both related to their dependence upon profits and upon the rate of profit.

Let us start with the first feature, assuming that under the influence of a special event (such as product innovation) investment decisions and—after a time lag—investment outlays increase. According to the multiplier principle, national income increases more strongly than investment while profits increase *pari passu* with investment. If profits stimulate investment, further investment decisions are to be expected and investment tends to increase cumulatively. This process is influenced by changes in the utilization of capacity and by changes in its size. With growing aggregate output, the degree of utilization of capacity grows, creating new stimuli for investment necessary to adjust capacity to an expanding aggregate output. Behind this development lies the well-known acceleration principle. On the other hand, the growth of investment and subsequently of the productive capacity itself creates a countertendency to the increasing degree of capacity utilization. Therefore the increase in capacity and in the degree of its utilization would influence the speed of the cumulative tendency of investment in an unpredictable way, strengthening or weakening this movement.

Of course, all the interconnections presented above might act in an opposite direction as well. If investment decisions and consequently investment outlays decrease they will tend to decrease cumulatively, and this movement will be influenced in an unpredictable manner by the changes in capacity and in the degree of its utilization.

The instability, the second feature of the analysed investment process, is related to the fact that a reverse movement of investment begins as soon as the cumulative movement comes to a stop. Let us assume that the contradictory process of changes in capacity and the degree of its utilization brings a cumulative increase of investment to a halt at a relatively high level (surpassing at least the level of depreciation). With constant investment, profits are constant too, but capital stock increases because net investment is positive. Thus the rate of profit, although high, starts to decrease and initiates a decline in investment. Or, for analogous reasons, the cumulative fall of investment comes to a halt at a relatively low level (below the depreciation level). With constant investment, profits are constant too, but capital stock decreases because net investment is negative. Thus the rate of profit, although low, starts to increase and initiates a rise in investment.

So far we have explaind the halt in the cumulative movement of investment by internal factors alone. But apart from this, some external factors would operate as a brake anyway. For instance, further increase in investment may be impossible because of full utilization of capacity in sector 1, or because of some other bottlenecks which sooner or later must appear in the course of a cumulative expansion in investment. The same applies to a cumulative decline in investment, because gross investment cannot become negative. If investment's movement is halted at a relatively high or low level because of external factors, the reverse movement begins in the manner described above and for the same reasons. In other words, under the assumed conditions investment cannot remain constant either at a relatively high or a relatively low level.

Thus we come to the conclusion that investment determined by firms reacting to market signals would fluctuate, and so would profits. If, as assumed earlier, the price/cost ratio in MS were to remain constant (or sticky), the fluctuations in profits would be passed to national income. With fluctuating national income, employment would fluctuate too. Even if in the boom full employment were attained, it could not be sustained in other phases of the business cycle—and the more so if full employment were not reached in the boom. Thus, averaged over the cycle, unemployment seems unavoidable in MS exposed to the influence of spontaneous market forces.

It should be stressed again that our results depend crucially on assumptions concerning the behaviour of the firm in MS. If this behaviour were to be different, because the budget constraint were in reality not hard enough, the demand of firms for investment would not be limited by profitability considerations only and their resistance to unjustified money wage claims would be weak. Under these conditions, resources would be overused and shortages and inflationary pressures (as customary in a CPE) would be unavoidable. Sooner or later central controls of investment and the wage bill would have to reappear, putting an end to the very concept of MS.

On the other hand, hardly any market system, and certainly not the market in contemporary capitalist economies, operates in a *laissez-faire* manner, that is without any state intervention aimed at modifying or mitigating some manifestations of market coordination judged harmful from the macroeconomic and/or social point of view. The question of compatibility of such intervention with the principle of market coordination is among the most controversial in economics. Having declared ourselves as followers of the Keynes-Kalecki approach to economic dynamics, our position is that there is considerable room for state intervention within the framework of a market system. This we regard as true not only in cases where the market fails altogether (which justify placing certain type of activity outside market coordination, to form what we call the 'non-enterprise sector') but also for the main sphere of economic activity where market coordination should be dominant (the 'enterprise sector'). Thus MS, as postulated here, need not be equated with a *laissez-faire* market system, and our picture of fluctuations caused by the investment behaviour of profit-pursuing firms ought to be supplemented by an analysis of the possible impact of state policies compatible with the concept of MS. In the next section of this chapter we shall discuss conventional macroeconomic policies, whereas in the fourth section the more complex and contentious issue of long-term growth and employment planning will be confronted.

MONETARY AND FISCAL POLICY — POSSIBILITIES AND LIMITS

Money will play an important role in MS. The monetary system will in MS—as mentioned already—consist of the central bank (CB) and commercial banks. The notes of the CB will represent the definitive means of payments (paper money) and they will be supplemented by deposit money created by the commercial banks, using paper money as their cash reserve. The sum of paper and deposit money outside the bank sector is usually defined as the quantity of money. This is a somewhat blurred definition; for example, some forms of savings could easily be included in the concept, and other means of payment (bills of exchange, money created by credit cards, and so on) rest outside the definition.

The supply of paper and deposit money will be controlled by the CB, and three most important tools of this control will probably (as in a capitalist system) consist of the following: open market operations, the minimal cash reserve ratio, and the rediscount rate. Through open market operations the CB buys and sells securities and hence increases and reduces the amount of paper money in the commercial banking system. Thus, given the minimal cash reserve ratio, the commercial banks can expand or contract the loan opportunities to the economy. Through changes in the minimal cash reserve ratio the CB can influence the quantity of deposit money, given the quantity of paper money. Last but not least, through changes in the rediscount rate, that is the rate at which the CB as the lender of last resort stands ready to lend to the commercial banks, it influences the rate of interest. The rate of interest depends, however, on open market operations too. Because an inverse relationship exists between the market price of securities and the current rate of interest, open market operations directly influence the latter. Thus the CB could, through control of the quantity of money, also influence the rate of interest. It is well known that in practice the CB when necessary, uses informal rationing of credits as well. There is no reason to exclude this possibility in MS either.

The demand for money is customarily split into three groups: transaction, precautionary, and speculative demand for money. The first two groups would quite certainly persist in MS and would be as everywhere, given payments habits, a function of national income. Indeed, as the receipts and expenditure of firms are not necessarily synchronized and the exact timing of both is not certain, the firms (and the households) would have to hold transaction balances of money. Balances will be held for various precautionary reasons related to unexpected bargain opportunities too. The situation is less clear in respect of the speculative demand for money. If, however, a secondary market for securities exists, as is postulated in many reform proposals, there is every reason for the development of the speculative demand for money also.

Let us assume that this is the case and firms are allowed to buy and sell securities on the secondary market. We shall treat all securities yielding fixed interest (government bonds, debentures issued by firms, and so on) as bonds, and view their price as inversely related to the current rate of interest. If firms are free to decide whether they hold money or bonds, the 'liquidity preference' theory would apply to them too. Let us assume that the rate of interest is such that the supply of bonds by holders who wish to sell equals the demand by those who wish to buy, while all other firms are satisfied with their holdings. The firms that hold speculative balances expect that the rate of interest will increase (that is the price of bonds will fall) and those that hold bonds expect that the rate of interest will decrease (the price of bonds will rise).

If now for some reason expectations change while the volume of speculative balances and bonds remain constant, the rate of interest will change without any changes in current savings or investment. Let us assume that the demand curve for speculative balances shifts to the right, which means at any given rate of interest that firms are willing to hold more speculative balances than previously. At the initial rate of interest the supply of bonds is now higher than demand for them; their price falls, and hence the rate of interest increases. This movement lasts till the market finds a new equilibrium at a higher rate of interest.

Thus changes in the rate of interest may occur without any changes in the volume of current savings and investment. On the other hand, the intention to save or invest more should not affect the rate of interest, and even when it does the impact is usually weak. Indeed, the demand for bonds coming from new savers, or the supply of bonds coming from new investors, represent a fraction only of the total bond market. If some firms intend to save and buy bonds there will be an increase in the price of bonds but only a slight one. The related slight fall in the interest rate could be sufficient to bring about an increase in the demand for speculative balances which would absorb the new savings. There will be only a small increase (or no increase at all) in investment. In this situation the intention to save more would not materialize. The volume of investment would remain more or less the same, with national income reduced if the rate of savings were to increase. The adjustment of national income and savings to given investment would follow under the circumstances the rules of the 'savings paradox'.

These are all well-known problems. They are repeated here in order to remind us that the rate of interest may be a poor tool for equating savings and investment in MS. This applies, in our opinion, to monetary policy in general. If the interest elasticity of demand for speculative balances is high and that of investment low, monetary policy will not be very effective; first, because changes in the quantity of money will not cause adequate changes in the rate of interest; and secondly, because the changes in the rate of interest will not be followed by adequate changes in investment. This would apply especially to periods of low economic activity: increasing liquidity and reducing the rate of interest may not be enough to stimulate economic activity if the mood of potential investors is pessimistic. On the other hand, keeping liquidity constant and raising the rate of interest may be quite successful when monetary policy aims to counter the overheating of the economy. This asymmetry may be of great practical relevance.

Most economists of the Keynes-Kalecki orientation tend to link the possibilities of influencing the level of economic activity with the tools of fiscal policy. We must thus complete our survey by a look at the role of government revenues and expenditures.

Let us assume that there exist government revenues from income tax on wages T_W and profits T_P (including social security payments net of transfer payments), and also current government expenditures G. The budget deficit D is the difference between government expenditures and revenues $(G-T_W-T_P)$. Thus we have on the one hand $Y = W + T_W + P + T_P$, and on the other $Y = C + I + G$, where P and W denote profits and wages, both after taxation. From the above equations we get $W + T_W + P + T_P = C + I + G$ and, because of our assumption $W = C$, we also get $P = I + G - T_W - T_P$. As $G - T_W - T_P$ is the budget deficit D, this means that $P = I + D$: profits (that is savings) of firms are equal to investment plus budget deficit. Thus, given the volume of firms' investment, the profits will be the higher as the budget deficit is higher. The national income will follow profits as shown in the second section of this chapter.

The budget deficit will move counter-cyclically if government expenditures follow their normal pace independent of revenues. Indeed, with increasing national income, tax revenues will increase too (the more so as transfer payments for the unemployed fall) and hence the budget deficit will be reduced. With falling national income the situation will be reversed. Therefore profits will go up and down but not as strongly as investment, resulting in national income fluctuations less pronounced than those of investment. This effect is due to the existence of the income-dependent tax and acts as a built-in stabilizer. The more progressive is the income system, the more powerful is the built-in stabilizer.

The role of the budget as a tool for control of the economy is not limited to deficit spending alone. Even with a balanced budget the national income will be stimulated to grow if an increase in government expenditures is financed by a parallel increase in taxes on profits, under the conditions that the price/cost ratio (implying a constant relation between profits *before* taxation and wages) remains constant. Indeed, denoting by P_B the profits before taxation we have

$$P_B = P + T_P = I + G\text{-}T_W$$

If now government expenditures increase by dG and the taxes on profits by $dT_P = dG$ we get

$$dP_B = dP + dT_P = dI + dG\text{-}dT_W$$

If we assume further $dI = dT_W = 0$ we have

$$dP_B = dP + dT_P = dG$$

and because of the assumed equality $dT_P = dG$ we have $dP = 0$ and $dP_B = dG$. This means that profits before taxation increase by the amount of the increase in government expenditures, and the increased tax on profits leaves profit after taxation unchanged. If now—as assumed—the price/cost ratio remains constant, the consumption of workers increases together with profits before taxation, that is with government expenditures. Indeed, $dY = dW + dP + dT_W + dT_P$, and $dY = dT_P + dW$ or $dY = dG + dC$ because $dP = dT_W = 0$, $dT_p = dG$, and $dW = dC.$[9]

The conclusion arrived at depends on two assumptions. First, it has been tacitly assumed that investment does not suffer from the increased taxation of profits. This assumption is based on the fact that investment outlays in a given period are an outcome of investment decisions in the preceding period; thus they remain given in the period under consideration and result in profits net of taxation which have not suffered from the increased tax on profits. Hence, if firms do not change their investment decisions immediately after the tax increase, they will not have an incentive to do so in the future either. On the other hand, however, the rate of interest must increase if the rate of interest net of taxation is to remain unchanged. This would lead to the reduction of profitability of new investment projects net of taxation and net of interest payments and, indeed, negatively affect the propensity to invest unless some other factors (such as an increase in the degree of capacity utilization) are sufficiently counteractive. Secondly, we have assumed that the increased taxes are not passed on to prices through an increase in the price/cost ratio. If they are, real wages and consumption out of wages suffer, and the outcome with regard to the volume of national income becomes indeterminate. For these reasons, financing of additional government expenditures through additional taxes on profits, although quite efficient, is not free from certain risks.

It should be mentioned that an increase in government expenditures financed by an increase in taxes on wages would leave the national income unchanged because the increase in government expenditures would be compensated by an equal decrease in workers' consumption.

The overall conclusions are that fiscal and—to a lesser degree—monetary policies should be able in MS to attenuate cyclical fluctuations and unemployment. If the budget shows a deficit in the depression and a surplus in the boom but remains balanced over the business cycle, no long-term problem of public debt arises. Even if this is not the case and the budget is in deficit over the cycle as a whole, the debt will not present special difficulties, provided that the relation of the volume of the debt to national income does not grow continuously. What may become a problem under these circumstances is the increase in taxes necessary for financing interest payments on public debt; it often happens that such tax increases are resisted. This has also some redistributive implications because it means that a portion of income collected in increased taxes goes to the receivers of interest on public debt. Otherwise, under the aforementioned conditions, public debt does not create an additional burden upon future generations.

In the case of a balanced budget over the business cycle, no additional effective demand is generated but profits fluctuate less. As they are expected to be the main factor influencing investment decisions in MS, it may well be that under these conditions fluctuations of investment itself would become less pronounced too. This is the paramount effect which can be expected from a successful anticyclical fiscal policy, supported when necessary by measures of monetary policy.

In reality the situation may, and surely would, become much more complicated. The rate of growth of national income over the cycle can change. If, for example, the long-run rate of growth of national income falls and the rate of growth of the public debt increases, or even remains constant, the ratio of public debt to national income grows, and the relative burden of the public debt rises quickly. Another source of difficulties may be related to an unexpected rise in the rate of interest and its influence upon servicing the public debt. It is clear that all these problems can occur in MS, leading to serious complications. Nevertheless, our analysis—despite its oversimplifications—has shown that an appropriate policy may be a factor in attenuating cyclical fluctuations of aggregate output and employment without upsetting the MS framework. The question we face now is whether even such a tentative conclusion can be drawn in respect of long-run growth of national income and employment.

PLANNING FOR FULL EMPLOYMENT IN MARKET SOCIALISM

We must begin by recalling that MS—like a capitalist market economy—is a demand-determined system with its typical price/cost ratio inflexibility (see the second section of this chapter). The problems deriving from this inflexibility become particularly visible when we go beyond the pure business cycle and turn to the process of growth. As the normal case in MS would likely be that of cyclical fluctuations around a growing level of investment and national income in this section we shall disregard the fluctuations of economic activity altogether. Let us assume that the rate of growth of investment following market signals and cleared of fluctuations is constant; hence the growth rate of national income is constant too. It may be expected, taking into account the experience of capitalist economies, that this rate of growth will be higher the stronger is the stream of all kinds of innovations, promising higher profits and new markets. The intensification of technical progress should therefore also remain a major factor in the acceleration of growth in MS.

We shall assume that the rate of growth of labour productivity m is constant and determined by technical progress, the capital/output ratio over time remaining constant. This corresponds to the neutral type of technical progress as defined by Harrod and Kalecki.[10] Let the rate of growth of employment n be a constant, too. Thus the rate of growth of national income is $g = m + n$ and represents the trend beyond the cyclical fluctuations of national income. If we assume further, for the sake of simplicity, that the labour force, (given the participation rate) also grows at the rate n, then the rate of unemployment (the relation between unemployment and the labour force) remains constant. Full employment means under the circumstances a zero rate of unemployment. We want to find out the conditions under which full employment in MS can be attained and preserved.

We assume also that at time t there exists capital (stock) K sufficiently large to ensure full employment provided aggregate

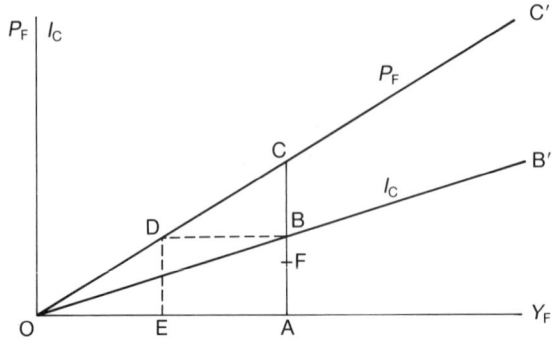

demand is adequate. We assume that at full employment the degree of utilization of existing capacity is optimal in the sense that it does not impair flexible adjustment of the structure of supply to that of the demand. Now, if at time t the aggregate demand were big enough, full employment with an optimal degree of utilization of capacity would be attained. The rate of growth of national income at full employment would be $g = m + n$, because on the one hand the rate of growth of labour productivity is determined by technical progress, and on the other (given the rate of growth of the labour force) a rate of growth of employment greater than n would cause labour shortages, and one smaller than n would result in unemployment. Under these conditions the volume of investment required to uphold the proper relation between capacity and national income at full employment must ensure a growth rate of capital equal to g. With an assumed constant capital/output ratio the capacity would then also grow at the rate g. Hence the degree of utilization of capacity would remain constant because national income and capacity would both grow at the rate g. We shall call this investment 'capacity-adjusted invest-ment', and denote it at the time t by $I_C = (g + a) K$, where a denotes the depreciation parameter.

In the accompanying figure we draw a line OB′ at a slope corresponding to the share of capacity-adjusted investment in full employment national income. Let full employment national income at time t be $Y_F = OA$ and let the capacity-adjusted investment at the same time be $I_C = AB$. The slope of OB′ corresponds to the rate of investment I_C/Y_F, which allows for capital growth at the rate g. Over time, national income at full employment moves along the abscissa, to the right of point A, and the capacity-adjusted investment moves along the line OB′, to the right of point B.

We draw now on the figure the line OC′ at the slope corresponding to the share of profits (that is savings) in the national income. We shall denote profits (savings) at full employment level as P_F. At time t, with national income $Y_F = OA$, full employment savings would amount to $P_F = AC$ and the share of savings in national income would be $s = (AC/OA)$. This share is determined by the existing price/cost ratio (given the savings propensities).

Let us assume that in the observed MS there exists some constant rate of unemployment. In terms of the figure this can be represented by a situation in which actual investment in time t corresponds to the segment AB; it is also assumed that this investment grows over time at the rate g. Thus capital and capacity grow at the rate g too. But given s, represented by the slope of the line OC′, actual national income at time t is $Y = OE$. Indeed, with investment AB savings amount to ED and national income is below its full employment level. If now investment grows, as assumed, at a rate g, so does national income. It remains however at a constant proportion below the full employment national income. The degree of utilization of capacity is, under these conditions, constant but lower than with full employment. Full employment must belong to the main economic policy objectives of the government in MS. So, what is to be done when the CPB, the body charged with the coordination of strategic economic decisions in MS, is confronted with the situation depicted in the figure? There exists a deflationary gap BC; in other words, the aggregate demand in the economy is insufficient. Under these conditions, should the CPB stimulate the investment decisions of the enterprise sector to level AC, thus closing the deflationary gap by additional investment? Let us say that this is done and that the stimuli used by the CPB can be represented by a reduction in the rate of interest. If investment is interest elastic then a reduction in the rate of interest would result in an increase in investment to level AC. In this way full employment is achieved but the rate of growth of capital and of capacity is higher than g because $AC > AB$, that is investment is higher than its capacity-adjusted level. This results in a reduction in the degree of capacity utilization, which in turn leads to a fall in the rate of profit. Indeed, while the capital stock grows at the rate higher than g, national income and (given the price/cost ratio) profits increase only at the rate g. Thus to sustain the initial stimulus the rate of interest would have to be continually cut in order to maintain the same level of profitability net of interest payments. The difference between the rate of profit and the rate of interest is the reward for risk taking and has to remain constant if the enterprise sector is expected to invest along the line CC′.[11]

It is true that if investment continues to grow at the rate g, sooner or later capital stock and capacity will adjust to this rate of growth too. From this moment on the rate of growth of capacity and of national income will reach g, and the degree of utilization of capacity will remain constant although at a lower level than the optimal one. This lower level of utilization of capacity will result in a lower rate of profit. Hence, the fall in the rate of interest comes to a stop but at a relatively low level which is necessary to compensate for the reduced rate of profit. The lower levels of utilization of capacity and of the rate of profit prove that superfluous investment has been undertaken. The purpose of investment is not to ensure full employment (the so-called 'income effect') but to create capacity (the so-called 'capacity effect'). One could say that useless spending on investment to ensure full employment is better than not spending enough, but rational spending on necessary capacity would obviously be preferable.

The theoretical example presented above—hopefully in a sufficiently clear manner—is meant to illustrate a general problem confronting the CPB in MS: the possibility of conflict between a given distribution of national income (the price/cost ratio) and the final use of national income, which is needed for securing both optimal utilization of capacities and full employment. The capacity-adjusted investment (AB in the figure) is what the economy needs to invest to keep capacities at the proper level at which they are properly utilized. But at the same time, savings (profits) may be available for the higher investment necessary to keep labour fully employed (AC > AB). If therefore investment is AB then unemployment is unavoidable, while if investment is AC then part of the productive capacity would remain idle, and hence part of the investment would be wasted. The CPB could under the circumstances attempt to reintroduce into MS an element of flexibility in the distribution of national income (price/cost ratio). However, when discussing the point in the second section, we indicated that such flexibility was ascribed to a centralized socialist economy in which some authority would fix both investment and prices in relation to money wages, that is costs. How can it be done without undermining the foundations of MS? This is the dilemma.

A solution might be sought along the lines of Kalecki's idea of instituting a general capital charge to be levied on every type of asset owned by firms, regardless of the degree of their liquidity—whether invested in new capacities, held in securities, or kept in a bank account.[12] This type of charge—independent of the actual perform- ance of firms in terms of profitability—is considered compatible with a market system. Let us examine how it may operate in MS, and what could be its contribution to maintaining long-term full employment.

The capital charge would constitute a revenue of the CBP, which would be entitled to use it at its own discretion according to macroeconomic considerations. The first priority of the CPB would be the attainment and preservation of full employment, but it could be given other tasks as well. In addition the level of capital charge would be left to the discretion of the CPB. It is perhaps worth while to note that, for instance, a capital charge of only 2 per cent per year with a capital/output ratio of 3 would put 6 per cent of national income at the disposal of the CPB.

The capital charge could be used for two main purposes: first, for paying a social dividend to all members of the society as the definitive owners of state firms; and secondly, for financing investment which cannot (or cannot properly) be undertaken by the enterprise sector itself. Investment in the 'non-enterprise' sector would pertain to broadly defined infrastructure. This applies first of all to investment in the infrastructure proper (related to the production of public goods), as well as to areas with pronounced external effects, where individual and short-term profitability are evidently a poor guide to efficiency. (Investment related to regional policy or to infant indus- tries may serve here as an example.) It should be stressed, however, that the direct investment of the CPB would have to remain a well- justified exception and not a rule, if the very sense of MS was to be preserved.

By collecting and dividing the capital charge between these two categories of expenditures, the CPB, without endangering the sover- eignty of firms, obtains an important tool for influencing the final use of national income, given the distribution between profits and wages as determined by the price/cost ratio. If for example the CPB were faced with the situation depicted in the figure, and if the capital charge were set at a level equal to the segment FC while investment of firms happened to reach exactly the level AF, then full employment would be simply secured by using the whole of the capital charge for social dividend payments (equal to the segment BC) and or invest- ment by the state in the non-enterprise sector (equal to the segment

FB). If investment by firms was bigger than AF, the CPB could cut its own spending out of capital charge in order to adjust the aggregate demand to the full employment national income. With the capital charge given, this would mean that a part of it would be saved, and in this form finance the overinvestment of the enterprise sector.

If, on the other hand, investment by firms was smaller than AF, then the spending of the CPB should be expanded beyond the segment FC; with the capital charge given, this would mean that the CPB becomes for a while a net borrower. However, in either of the two cases of discrepancy between the desired and actual levels of investment of the enterprise sector, manipulation of the structure of expenditures out of capital charge may prove in itself insufficient. Monetary policy (raising or reducing interest rates) and fiscal incentives or disincentives for investment would have to be used, and in extreme situations perhaps even such measures as investment licensing.

An important instrument for encouraging the investment activity of firms could be a change in the level of the capital charge. Let us consider the problem for a moment. With a balanced state budget, profits (after taxation) $P = I + E$, where E, denotes the expenditures of the CPB on social dividend and/or state investment. Indeed, assuming—as previously—no savings out of private households, profits are determined now both by the investment of firms and by the expenditures of the CPB. If the capital charge on the enterprise sector amounts to E, profits net of capital charge (that is, the savings of firms) are equal to I. If the CPB increases both the capital charge and its expenditures by dE, profits increase by $dP = dE$, assuming that investment by the enterprise sector remains unchanged. This will indeed be the case directly after the increase in the capital charge because of the time lag between investment outlays and decisions. But even current investment decisions should not be negatively influenced by the increase in the capital charge, because this increase does not reduce the profitability of investment financed either from own or from borrowed sources. The principle of the capital charge—levied on all assets regardless of their degree of liquidity—means that the charge would have to be paid even if a firm refrained from investment. And if a firm finances investment by credit, its own capital does not increase, and the decision to invest does not involve higher charges. Moreover, because profits (including capital charge) increase by dP, and the profitability of investment measured by P rises, the expectations of firms regarding future profitability should improve and a higher propensity to invest may be expected. In the same direction acts the increase of national income dY (and of consumption dC) caused by the rise of profits (including capital charge), and it leads to a higher degree of capacity utilization. It seems therefore that an increase in the capital charge can turn out to be a promising tool to stimulate firms' investment activity.[13]

Generally speaking, capital charge should be fixed at a level at which the CPB is able to balance expenditures with revenues in the long run. But the CPB could also deviate from this rule by using a surplus or a deficit of capital charge over expenditures as a tool of indirect incomes policy. If for example, the existing share of profits in national income was judged as proper, but a shift in the price/cost ratio would tend to change this share, the mechanism of surplus or deficit spending out of capital charge could act as a countervailing factor. Thus, when the price/cost ratio was to increase (pushing up the share of profits in national income), social dividend could be raised to support consumption in order to secure full employment. With the level of capital charge given, the CPB would become a net borrower. Again, this in itself would hardly solve the problem, but might provide the CPB with a breathing space for developing policies aiming at lowering the price/cost ratio (for example by supporting trade unions' pressure for higher wages, or, in an extreme case, by some form of price control). If the price/cost ratio were to decrease as a result of the growth of money wages exceeding the growth of labour productivity (with given prices), then social dividend could be cut to counteract inflationary pressure. With the level of capital charge given, the CPB would now become a net saver. Here, again other measures would have to be taken to push up the price/cost ratio to an acceptable level.

Needless to say, the mechanism described above might bring some results only within a limited range of rather short—or medium-term phenomena. Should the price/cost ratio display a long-run tendency to grow, the capital charge would have *ceteris paribus* to increase as well, in order to compensate for the too slow rise of money wages with a faster increase in the social dividend. Conversely, in the case of the price/cost ratio displaying a long-run tendency to fall, the capital charge would have to be reduced correspondingly. Should, however, the latter trend continue indefinitely, the capital charge would ultimately vanish altogether, leaving the CPB unable to finance even its investment any more. Thus the condition of the effectiveness of the system would be a long-term incomes policy securing a share of profits in national income higher than the share of capacity-adjusted investment at full employment level. Besides, a long-run tendency to reduce the price/cost ratio would be a reflection of the fact that firms are unable to resist the money wage demands of the workforce, and that their budget constraint is not really hard.

CONCLUSION

The upshot of our analysis is that an effective policy of long-run full employment may be possible in MS. At the same time this analysis shows—we hope sufficiently clearly—how qualified such an answer must be. First, even under very simplified assumptions, the CPB in its pursuit of long-term full employment cannot rely merely on the non-enterprise sector and on indirectly influencing the enterprise sector (with the capital charge as its main instrument), but is required time and again to consider the need for direct action (investment licensing, price controls, incomes policy). This, by the way, adds substance to the traditional name of CPB for the body coordinating strategic economic decisions in MS: its activities and time horizon may justify the adjective 'planning', although its meaning is fundamentally different from that pertaining in countries of 'real socialism'.

Secondly, every step towards relaxation of our simplified assumptions opens up a whole new sphere of problems and presents difficulties of great (many would say, dramatic) complexity. We have assumed, for instance, that the rate of growth used for defining the level of capacity-adjusted investment is given. In actual fact this rate will usually change, particularly in the short run, but sometimes in the long run as well. One source of such instability might be a change in the rate of growth of labour productivity under the influence of changes in the capital/output ratio (or in the lifespan of equipment, or in both) in the short and medium term, and—depending on the type of technical progress—even in the long run. These changes might be quite complicated, such as an acceleration followed by a deceleration in growth, and vice versa. Even without changes in the capital/output ratio or in the lifespan of equipment, the rate of growth of labour productivity is likely to change because of the unpredictability of the variations in intensity of technical progress. The other basic component of growth—increase in the labour force,—cannot be taken as stable either. The rate of growth of population fluctuates, and even when these variations are negligible the participation ratio and/or the length of the work period might change, and so on. An important problem of another kind may arise when the task of achieving full employment is being undertaken not in a situation of inadequate aggregate demand but under conditions of scarcity of capital in relation to the existing labour force. All the factors mentioned would exert a meaningful impact on the share of capacity-adjusted investment, which we have assumed in our analysis as constant. Even without going into the matter further, it should be abundantly clear that the CPB would face quite a problem in getting its calculations right and in adjusting its policies appropriately. Should we move from a closed economy, as considered throughout our analysis, to an open one, the problem would be not simply compounded, but raised on to a qualitatively different level of difficulty: not only would forecasting become much more intricate, but also the freedom of action of the CPB would come up against severe limitations.

An obvious response of those who see MS as relief from the pains of 'real socialism' would be to point out that the difficulties indicated above arise mostly from the formidable requirement to combine in MS microefficiency with macrostability to secure long-term full employment. In a capitalist market economy a government set on such economic policy objectives would confront similar obstacles, or even greater, for instance because of political barriers to the use of a capital charge in a private market economy. All this is true. However, in the shape discussed so far, MS has a heavy burden of its own which has been skimmed over in this chapter: we assumed that enterprises (firms), although publicly (state) owned, will behave exactly as their capitalist counterparts, displaying the same level of microeconomic efficiency and the same alertness to opportunities offered by technical progress and by changes in the parameters of the system. This assumption must be tested before any further conclusions can be drawn.

IO

The Question of Ownership

The question which has to be answered in the process of testing the assumption underlying our analysis in Chapter 9 can be formulated simply in the following way: is MS—requiring full independence of firms and true entrepreneurship—compatible with the dominant position of public (state) ownership of the means of production?

With the benefit of hindsight it becomes clear that the problem of ownership should have been raised earlier, namely when the model of 'central planning with regulated market' was on the agenda. Even the devolution of the so-called current or standard economic decisions from the centre to enterprises was supposed to create for the latter some degree of autonomy, and thus should pose the question whether and how this autonomy can be reconciled with the unchanged status of state-owned enterprises. When one of the present authors discussed the problem of ownership in the early 1970s, he concentrated instead on the postulated socialization of state ownership through democratization of the political system, a process which was also thought to enhance the efficiency of the investment decisions taken by the state, and hence provide the rationale for keeping them at the central level.[1]

Although the political factor remains important for MS, the main focus in the context of our analysis shifts to the problem of compatibility: are state-owned firms capable of fully fledged market behaviour? We deal with that problem in this chapter, but we have no ambitions to discuss general issues of ownership theory. Our interest is limited to those aspects which bear directly on the operational conditions for MS, and even within these confines we shall omit a number of areas, such as the emerging forms of transnational ownership (joint ventures).

Our starting point is the 'traditional' state enterprise of the Soviet type, re-enacted after 1945 virtually without change in all countries of 'real socialism'. If, following Holešovsky,[2] substantive ownership rights or the practical content of ownership are defined as consisting of rights of custody, usufruct, alienation, and destruction, it could be said that in the command system the 'traditional' state-owned enterprise enjoyed none of these; all were unambiguously vested in organs of state administration (we disregard here the relationshp between the state administration and the political rulers). The change towards MS must therefore mean first, that most of these rights must be renounced by the state administration in favour of the state enterprise; and secondly, that the latter must be capable of making use of them. Both points will be discussed in turn.

At first glance it might seem convenient to discuss the first point— how ownership rights are to be shifted from the state administration to the state enterprise—in the familiar terms of the divorce between ownership and control. But 'control' in general is actually a vague concept, and when it becomes more specific and located within custody rights (the right to determine how to use assets, that is the right to manage) it covers part of the ownership rights themselves by the definition adopted above. Moreover, the two main theoretical camps in the substantive dispute on private *versus* public ownership actually share a belief in the infeasibility of the divorce between ownership and control. Marxist social theory has at its core the proposition that he who owns ultimately controls,[3] and any attempt to put this proposition in doubt was always strenuously refuted by Marxists; here lies probably the intellectual source of the untouchability of public ownership as the cornerstone of socialism. Symmetrically, the ideologists of the free private market economy were equally adamant that control cannot be divorced from ownership; hence the untouchability of private ownership as the cornerstone of the market. For the protagonists of the 'property rights school', any degree of even managerial (let alone entrepreneurial) independence from shareholders' control in a corporate setting is tantamount to attenuation of the substance of ownership.[4]

We will probably be unable to avoid the convenient catch-all term 'control' in our discussion, but we shall try wherever possible to be more specific, and particularly to take into account the distinction most important in our case (or so we think), namely that between ownership, management, and entrepreneurship.

The command system engenders a peculiar unity of ownership, management, and entrepreneurship (the last designation is likely to be questioned by some as in principle inapplicable to the command economy). The state administration managed the use of enterprises' assets by prescribing all elements of their activity (custody rights); the state budget appropriated the residual returns (usufruct); no part of enterprises' assets could be sold or passed over to any other entity without the explicit instruction (or at least the consent) of the state administration (alienation rights); and destruction of such assets was controlled most meticulously when it was authorized, and was obviously regarded as a severe crime when it was not. It goes without saying that all these rights fully covered entry and exit, that is the establishment and closing down of enterprises. This peculiar unity of ownership, management, and entrepreneurship could and in practice had to be broken by actions which went against the rules (we do not here have in mind stealing from the state, which is a change in possession, but activities bending the regulations for the benefit of the system).

Already the reform concepts of 'central planning with regulated market', the initial design of the Hungarian NEM included, had somewhat undermined this unity. The state was expected to shift some part of its custody rights from the administration to the management—whatever its structure (the problem of organizational forms will be taken up later in this chapter). In other respects, however, the previous position and the scope of state ownership had hardly been challenged, with the exception of Yugoslavia. Moreover, strenuous efforts were made to show that no changes in ownership rights were involved by the reform in the state sector. In a slightly different but related context this position was expressed *inter alia* by the distinguished Soviet economist V. V. Novozhilov, who argued that what was at stake in the reform was not renunciation of centralized control, but replacement of direct centralization by an indirect one, more flexible and more conducive to efficiency while at the same time more comprehensive.[5] To some extent this might have been dictated by tactical considerations. However, the substantive element should not be overlooked; the state administration relinquished control over the details of the use of enterprises' productive capacity, but the financial means of 'parametric management' were still to secure the overall conformity of outcome with the stipulations of the central plan; the latter was called to reflect the centre's preferences with regard to the physical structure of the economy as well, albeit in more aggregate terms than under the command system. The dominant role of the state administration in investment decisions, particularly those underlying the creation of new enterprises, was the crucial component of the instrumental approach to the 'regulated market', and at the same time a reflection of the basically unchanged way of exercising state ownership rights.

MS requires precisely such fundamental change. Full custody

rights must be located in the enterprise itself. Not only current problems but also the entire complex of issues connected with investment activity are to be decided here, including—what is perhaps most important—the distribution of value added between wages and profits, and the choice between investing in physical assets and purely financial ones. An enterprise must be given alienation rights as well: it is indisputable that it can change the form of assets (for instance, selling off some part of productive capacity and keeping the proceeds in money form), and moreover it is hard to see why it should be prevented from sacrificing a part of the net value of assets as well if that's justified by sound business considerations, especially in the longer run. Furthermore, under competitive conditions a change in the value of capital is an element of the process of the rise and fall of firms; therefore an imitation of the formally binding rule in Yugoslavia, where the self-managed entities are granted custody rights to a given fraction of 'social capital' under the condition of maintaining its initial value, does not look viable. As for the usufruct rights, they have to be shared: putting it in its simplest terms, profits (after tax) go to the enterprise, fixed return on capital (and/or land, natural resources, and so on) to the state. The minimum return on capital ought to be paid both on initial and on accumulated own capital (see Chapter 9), making the state interested in an increase of the value of assets; the stimulus for an enterprise to increase the value of assets comes through profitability.

The emerging picture, its oversimplifications notwithstanding, is plain enough to make one realize how contradictory the requirements of our MS are. On the one hand, the position of the enterprise is different in kind from that under the 'regulated market', let alone under the command system; the postulated degree of independence of the enterprise is tantamount to acquisition of most of the ownership rights. On the other hand the enterprise is to remain *state owned*, which implies that the state retains the status of principal, keeping the ultimate power of control over the enterprise, whose management remains in the position of an agent acting on the principal's behalf and hence in a dependent position. Taken to the extreme, there is a conflict here which cannot be resolved: *full* independence of an enterprise is incompatible with state ownership, or any other external ownership for that matter. The only question worth examining in the context of MS is, therefore, the viability of the compromise solution of sharing ownership rights, as sketched above.

The core of this solution is the renunciation by the state of all interest and involvement in enterprises' activity, except the return on and growth of assets. This in turn presupposes a firm *separation* between a number of roles hitherto performed by the socialist state in such close interconnection that they have come to be regarded as indivisible: the role of the owner state should be separated from the state as an authority in charge of administration, national defence, and public order, entitled by law to impose taxes and duties; from the state as a regulatory body, setting business, health, safety, and other standards; from the state as the centre of macroeconomic policy, conventional and beyond (Chapter 9); and from the state as the organ of social and infrastructural policy, dealing with objectives and the means to achieve them, which cannot be defined in ordinary profit-and-loss terms (public goods, externalities). The last must lead to a separation of the (state) enterprise sector from the non-enterprise sector, which operates under the presumption that in this area the otherwise unavoidable government failures are as a rule less damaging than the market ones.

This is a formidable list of requirements, daunting under any conditions. Additionally it has to be noted—without entering into the whole complexity of the issue—that such separation presents enormous political problems as far as the transition from 'real socialism' to MS is concerned. The economy has to become depoliticized, that is free of the *nomenklatura* system of appointments and dismissals; free of the superior position of the Communist Party apparatus and executive bodies to that of the economic management and formally elected state organs; and free of the disregard for the rule of law binding equally the individual and the state, as a side in contracts, as a tax authority, as an economic policymaker. Moreover, depoliticization of the economy must be accompanied by democratization (or, in the terms we prefer, pluralization) of the polity, because no other guarantee can meaningfully exist for the maintenance of the depoliticization of the economy, and especially of the genuine rule of law (*Rechtsstaat*) indispensable for the normal operation of a market mechanism. The very notion of the all-powerful state, claiming its right to arbitrary actions as an embodiment of public interest, must therefore give way under MS to a concept of the economic role of the state as one of the actors, obliged—along with the others—to adhere to the rules. Furthermore, in its role as an authority, the duty of the state is to guard the rights to economic activity required by MS and to prevent their abuse.

Returning now to the enterprise sector itself, another vital separation must occur under MS: state enterprises (we use this designation regardless of the scale of agglomeration) have to become separated not only from the state in its wider role but also from each other. Enterprises have to behave as separate entities, not merely for account and organizational reasons as under the command system, or as under the 'regulated' market system within the area of activity determined for them by the central investment decisions supposed to be taken directly on the basis of some aggregate preference function, but in a full-blooded economic sense. They have to be competitive—rivals or allies depending on circumstances, merging or taking over, all from the point of view of the distinct interests of each of them. This poses a new, hardly mentioned, problem for the very concept of state ownership: fragmentation of state ownership as such into a conglomeration of parts, each of which stands on its own. The position is unlike that of a large private corporation which may judge each individual division by its contribution to overall results, may engage in cross-subsidization if it pays off by aggregate criteria, and so on. The difference lies in the specific weight of the sum total of state enterprises in the economy (the enterprise sector) as a whole: even under conditions of oligopolistic competition a large corporation still acts in a market environment and cannot destroy the principal rules of the game, whereas—under conditions of dominance of state-owned enterprises—a concerted action by the criterion of profitability of the totality of state assets would actually destroy the market and let in the command system by the back door. Thus, however paradoxical it may sound, unless the state's share in the enterprise sector becomes sufficiently small, the components of the state's domain must under MS be given greater autonomy than the divisions of a private corporation. The designation 'USSR Inc.' (or any other communist country, for that matter), used with such relish by some Western scholars, proves therefore to be wrong not only in the case of the command system, but also in the case of MS, although for other reasons: in order to arrive at MS, the state must deliberately engineer fragmentation of its possession.

Needless to say, all this is a major departure from the original socialist idea of 'directly social labour', with its powerful stress on integration and cooperation as against separation and rivalry (see Chapter 1). The formula of state ownership of the means of production as 'ownership of the whole people' may have been used widely for propaganda purposes, but it reflected also the substantive concept of indivisibility of the object of public ownership,[6] at least on a national scale (the implications of the expected vanishing of national boundaries was never incorporated properly into Marxist ideas about the future society). The indivisibility of public ownership underlay the claim to the superior rationality of socialism as well as to the superiority of state ownership compared with any kind of ownership involving separation: collective (cooperative), or even that of state authorities but on a local level and hence separated (municipal ownership). It is worth noting that along with pressure for the independence of state enterprises in the course of economic reforms, attitudes have become more favourable towards municipal ownership and cooperatives. The latter have slowly gained recognition, not only as a bridge through which smallholders (particularly peasants, as in Lenin's 'cooperative plan') will reach the ultimate of public ownership, but as a legitimate constant component of a socialist economy.

Thus the MS compromise solution demands separation of the state as owner from the state as an authority, regulatory body, and custodian of the non-enterprise sector, as well as separation of the state-owned enterprises from each other. There is no precedent for such a separation, and it would be an understatement to say that it would be difficult to attain. But even so, assuming that it has happened, the owner state must be entitled to exercise right of control over the enterprises in matters concerning their financial performance, particularly with regard to the relation of the actual performance to the potential one. Were this right denied, hardly anything would be left of state ownership; enterprises would be in the position of having full (but ill-defined) ownership rights, with the only obligation being to pay a charge on assets.

Of course, the case for separation of the state from enterprises cannot be taken as tantamount to barring direct state intervention under all circumstances. Practice is always richer than models, and there will be situations, in the enterprise sector as well, when such intervention may prove indispensable. However, our concern here is with the rule and not with the inevitable deviations.

We now turn to our second point, namely, the feasibility of a state enterprise behaving as a fully fledged market player, provided all the above requirements of separation are met. We consider first an enterprise endowed with most of the ownership rights and hence with the necessary degree of independence, but still ultimately controlled by the state. Can such an enterprise be said to operate under the same kind of budget constraint and the same conditions for entrepreneurship as a private firm?

In the light of past experience the answer would seem obvious: no. However, this experience cannot be taken yet as sufficient empirical evidence because state enterprises have never actually found themselves under the conditions postulated for MS. In addition the well-known fact that, in countries which have progressed in economic reform, it has been not the state enterprises but the private and cooperative ones which have taken most advantage of the modified system, provides in itself no overwhelming evidence either, because the latter were given freedom of action while the former were not. The post-1965 Yugoslav experience with 'social' enterprises might have come closest to corroborating the negative answer if it were not for the overall peculiarities of the Yugoslav case, especially the self-management form of enterprises and the fragmentation of the national market, which make it hardly suitable for generalization. The experience of nationalized enterprises in Western market economies is not unambiguous either: first, alongside unsuccessful public companies there are also (admittedly less numerous) examples to the contrary (Volkswagen may be cited as one of them); secondly, poor performance is blamed by some analysts not on public ownership of companies as such but on incorrect government policies and mistaken organizational forms.[7] Somewhat ironically it might be said that the latter point found a paradoxical corroboration in the improvement in performance of public companies in Britain when in the runup to privatization the Thatcher Conservative Government hardened the budget constraint, to use again Kornai's term, and forced nationalized industries to become respectably profitable.

Should we agree on the inconclusivity of past experience, the answer to our question must be sought in hypothetical—one might say speculative—reasoning. Let us start by comparing the position of a manager (chief executive) of a state enterprise with that of a manager of a private one, when the latter is not an owner or a co-owner (shareholder) of the company. At first sight, assuming that the state strictly adheres to the separation rules indicated above, the socialist manager's behaviour ought not to differ in principle from that of his corporate counterpart. His objective function is the same, and he is assessed by the same criteria. An appropriate bundle of incentives—career prospects at stake, high salary, bonuses or penalties depending on performance, pension rights, length of contracts, and so on—should engender appropriate motivation. Provided that ideological obstacles to the required income differentials are removed (this has to be regarded as indispensable under MS) there is apparently nothing impossible about devising an incentives scheme for managers of state enterprises operating under conditions of uncertainty.[8] Should this be the case, socialist managers ought to be sensitive to costs, market shares, profit, capital gains, and so on to no lesser degree than hired professional managers of capitalist enterprises. Probably the most difficult for socialist managers would be the area of wages and hence labour costs. The evident failure of virtually all 'automatic' wage control formulas proposed so far in the course of economic reforms, including (or perhaps even in particular) those based on self-management, seems to indicate that MS would have to re-create, to open up the contradictory character of wage bargaining. Recognition of conflict within state enterprises instead of the promised harmony may be not only awkward ideologically but also very intricate to handle in practice when, behind managerial resistance to what is regarded as excessive wage demands, there stands the state with all its resources. Nevertheless, in this respect too the difference between state and private management need not be so great—of course, under the stipulation that the state as owner firmly holds its ground and does not bail out firms lax in wage expenditures.

The real problem is with entrepreneurship—the area of 'creative destruction', of high risk and uncertainty. Distinguishing between management and entrepreneurship amounts perhaps to hair splitting; however, it may be useful to stress in the former the administration of entrusted resources and the reactions to the changing environment, whereas in the latter it is the grasping of new opportunities, hitherto unknown and not realized properly by others until now, that first comes to mind. As a rule entrepreneurial qualities are required from the top management of private corporations, but this does not invalidate the distinction beween the roles.

Is a socialist manager likely to be successful in the role of an entrepreneur? It is not so much the lack of motivation which puts that in doubt. After all, he may be stimulated sufficiently by a feeling of duty, or ambition, as well as by material gains, although probably not by the prospect of amassing such personal wealth as may be the case with his capitalist counterpart. What he will be mainly lacking, however, is the material foundation of responsibility for risks when the venture fails. He does not risk his own capital, and this, as emphasized by Hayek long ago,[9] makes it highly probable that he will err either on the side of recklessness or on the side of overcautiousness.

This is familiar stuff; but can it not be helped by bringing the entrepreneurial function closer to the ultimate owner? The link between entrepreneurship and ownership in modern capitalism is still a contentious issue, although the supporters of the divorce of control from ownership along the lines of Burnham's 'managerial revolution'[10] have become less vocal towards the end of the twentieth century. This is not to say that what may be called 'managerial corporations', in which the managers and not the owners perform the entrepreneurial function, do not exist, but it seems to us that these are by far the less typical cases. In order to assess properly the relationship between ownership and entrepreneurship in large capitalist joint stock companies, one has to distinguish between the mass of dispersed shareholders and perhaps some categories of institutional investors on the one hand, and the owners of large chunks of capital, controlling the company or at least capable of challenging for control through takeover bids, on the other. The former do not exercise entrepreneurial functions; they behave rather like rentiers interested in dividends and capital gains only, passing their judgement on the entrepreneurship and management of the company through acquisition or disposition of shares in the market. The latter—the controlling or almost controlling owners—are the main carriers or potential carriers of the entrepreneurial function through direct strategic decisions taken by the boards of directors, through supervision of the management actions, and through personnel policy. Here one can hardly claim a divorce between ownership and entrepreneurship: the acquisition of the controlling stake serves essentially the purpose of providing the owner with the opportunity to reveal his entrepreneurial talents (and luck). Needless to say, the connection between ownership and entrepreneurship in the world of corporate capitalism usually runs through a maze of intermediate links, but on the bottom line the element of individual risk is as a rule traceable to the owner, and the degree of responsibility for losses stands in some proportion to the degree of control over the company.

Could it work similarly in the case of the state being the ultimate owner in the sense used above? It is difficult to see how. Let us say that the government, in accordance with its purely financial objectives under MS, entrusts the task of supervision of managerial activities to one of its departments (the treasury, because branch ministries have no place in MS), or to a specially created enterprise board (or boards). The members of such treasury bodies or enterprise boards are representatives of the owner state; they exercise control over management (including, obviously, personnel matters), they take strategic decisions on their own or on the management's initiative, and they assess the risks involved. In short, they come as close as possible to the position of the controlling owners of a private corporation in terms of power—but not in terms of responsibility embedded in their own material stake. In the latter respect they remain like agents—as the hired managers are—charged by some body higher up in the hierarchy to fulfill given tasks (however widely defined), evaluated by the same bodies on criteria derived from these tasks, and stimulated by some kind of incentive scheme. The trouble is that most major decisions in a market environment contain, apart from routine components, unpredictable speculative elements, and it is these which are as a rule beyond the genuine capacity of an agent to handle. Nothing changes, of course, when even higher tiers of the hierarchy are created: the true principals—acting in their own name, and unable to pass responsibility for risks any further—are nowhere to be found in the anonymous state institutional structure. And it is this that makes it in the first place so difficult, or nigh impossible, to locate the entrepreneurial function in the framework of state owner-ship. In Chapter 1 we mentioned the Marxist assumption of the distinction between principals and agents fading away under social-ism because the 'quasi-principals' would show all the proper concerns for public good and willingness to take responsibility for risks. It goes without saying that the practice of 'real socialism' has proved to be light years removed from this assumption. But the point which we try to make here is that even with the appropriate socialist motivation the problem of entrepreneurship may remain unresolvable without anchoring responsibility for losses in personal stakes. Fully fledged market conditions resemble—if we may be excused the analogy—the game of poker, which can hardly be played without risking one's stake. Thus it is not so much the degree of personal competence, dedication, motivation, and taste for innovations, as the conditions forcing a principal to weigh the risks against responsibilities in a real world of uncertainty, which seem to draw the line distinguishing entrepreneurial from purely managerial behaviour. It looks, therefore, that even when the separation requirements discussed previously are fulfilled (in itself a tall order!) state enterprises can hardly be expected to become the same kind of players in the market as private—

individual or collective—enterprises. This applies particularly to the capital market strongly connected with investment in new ventures.

The hypothetical nature of the argument calls for restraint in the resoluteness of the conclusions. It would probably be an exaggeration to maintain that no horizontal financial intermediation, and hence no forms of capital market, are possible with state enterprises as the only participants. However, the actual benefits of the creation of a capital market under these conditions may fall considerably short of expectations, especially with regard to the equity market and its asset valuation functions. On the other hand, the instability consequences may well be strong.

Can a reorganization of the state enterprise sector change any of these conclusions? The matter deserves brief examination, as it is given plenty of attention in all countries of 'real socialism' trying to extend the scope of a market-oriented economic reform.[11]

A *state holding company*, advanced by a number of Hungarian economists, is supposed to be a purely financial institution exercising control over enterprises on the basis of full ownership of or a majority stake in their assets. It may have some advantages over a system of direct ownership of enterprises by the treasury: first, it may create a space between the enterprise sector and the politico-administrative authorities, helping the institutional side of the required separation; secondly, it may facilitate competition and the flow of capital between different branches of production; thirdly, it may open the possibility of transforming traditional state enterprises into joint stock companies in which shares are not owned exclusively by the state. Nevertheless, none of the problems indicated earlier seems to be substantially altered, let alone to disappear. Nothing at all changes in the substance of the principal-agent relationship when the state remains the only owner: the directors of the holding company to whom enterprise management is answerable are in turn answerable to some state organ, with the same kind of responsibility for risks. In the case of diversification of shareholding the scale of real change depends on the degree of freedom of access: if state entities only were allowed to buy shares, perhaps greater variety of direct interests might come to the fore in the decision-making process, but otherwise the position would remain as before because each of the shareholders would be still ultimately the agent of the state. Inclusion of institutional investors—pension funds, trade unions, and other voluntary organizations—provided that they are genuinely independent from the state, may create a welcome external element of control and pressure for better performance, both in the boardroom and particularly through 'voting with their feet', that is investing or disinvesting in the company's shares. If, however, the state's majority stake or another form of effective overall control is to be guaranteed as a manifestation of the state's ownership, this external element would still remain a subordinate factor. The role of private investors, were they to be allowed to become minority shareholders, should hardly help in this respect: private investors would probably be more sensitive to market movements in pursuit of financial gains, but at the same time less (if at all) effective in influencing the directors' decisions because of dispersion of shares. Thus the joint stock form of companies under state control cannot contribute much, in our opinion, to the solution of the problem of entrepreneurship.

The next form to be considered is a *self-managed* firm. This has been the mainstay of the Yugoslav idea of market socialism, and—in one way or another—is present in practice in all the more radical designs of economic reform in countries of 'real socialism', including the USSR. Characteristically, unlike the original NEM, it made in the 1980s a prominent appearance in Hungary, and the Polish reform slogan of 'the three Ss' (self-dependence, self-financing, self-management) illustrated well the perception of the close link between self-management and the push towards marketization of the economy. The Yugoslav experience, as indicated in Chapter 8, has shown however that—even independently of the X-efficiency factor—the link between self-management and entrepreneurial behaviour cannot be taken for granted. Whether self-management might create conditions for entrepreneurship seems again to depend critically on where ownership rights are located. The Yugoslav theory vested them in 'society', which in practice left them confused and frequently taken over by the state administration.[12] The Hungarian and the Polish reformers spoke of self-managed state enterprises, which openly expounded the position of the state as the owner; no individual property rights are assigned to the members of the workforce, who benefit or lose out in connection with performance only as long as they remain in the enterprise. If state ownership should mean anything in substance, the problems with a self-managed enterprise would look no different from those of the conventional ones.

However, the popularity of the self-management idea among the radical reformers, as transpired with particular strength in the programmatic documents of the Polish Solidarity movement in 1981 when the slogan of the 'self-managed republic' was launched, seems to stem from the belief that self-management might become an instrument for severing the subordination of the enterprise to the state. The main reflection of this severance was to be the right of a self-managed enterprise to elect its own management. Pushed to its logical conclusion, this way of using the self-management concept would lead to the full independence of the enterprise. But first such independence, as observed earlier, would leave the notion of state ownership meaningless; and secondly it would require a redefinition of the ownership rights of the workers' collective. Without individual stakes in capital, the collective as such actually becomes the holder of these rights; unless full and lasting identification of individual interests with that of the collective can be assumed, the bias against accumulation which is familiar from Yugoslav practice is likely to emerge as a rational behavioural principle. With individual stakes in capital, the self-managed enterprise changes, or starts to change, into a cooperative or a partnership. There is no point in speculating on the great variety of the possible transitionary or intermediate forms; in one way or another the direction in this case is clearly towards the institutionalization of the enterprise outside the confines of state ownership.

The recognition of the enormous difficulties in creating conditions propitious for entrepreneurship on the basis of state ownership are undoubtedly at the root of the proliferation of various concepts of *contracting out* state capital to individuals (families) or self-organized partnerships of individuals (families). The speed at which the cautious and strictly circumscribed initial ideas during the 1980s evolved into concepts close to long-term private leaseholds of land and capital is truly amazing. Evidently prompted by the early success of the Chinese 'production responsibility system' in agriculture, Gorbachev declared in March 1988 that 'collective and state farms should in the near future become in essence cooperative associations of financially independent contract groups', with the 'leasehold contract' to be regarded as the most appropriate.[13] This and similar statements in other countries of 'real socialism', accompanied by legal provisions and (in varying degree) by practical measures, seem to indicate that the concept is no longer applied to areas of activity looked upon as marginal (for instance, personal services), but has begun to be treated as a more general means to overcome the conflict between state ownership of productive resources and entrepreneurship. To put it crudely: the state retreats to the position of a passive beneficiary of its property, of some kind of rentier, ceding—against a contractual charge and acceptance of the normal conditions laid down by the freeholder, such as preservation of the value of the assets—all other ownership rights to the private (individual or group) leaser who becomes responsible for risks.

Private leaseholds of specified kinds of capital (and land), when sufficiently long term and undertaken with confidence in the legal stability of the system, open up the field for managerial initiative and entrepreneurship. But its scope is still limited by the very specificity of the capital: a lease on a state restaurant does not allow the leaseholder to move into information technology; even less so in the case of a franchise to produce and/or to market a specific product. That is why the search for a method to use state assets in an entrepreneurial way also generated a more comprehensive and certainly a more daring concept: the *entrepreneurial socialism* of the Hungarian economist Tibor Liska.[14] In entrepreneurial socialism the general principle is the auctioning of state assets for use by the highest bidders, who in turn are themselves subject to takeover unless they are prepared to match the higher bid. What mainly distinguishes this idea from ordinary leaseholds, apart from its generality, is the clear value orientation: no assignment to any specific area of activity, and full freedom to change physical forms of assets in a continuous competitive process of valuation. At the same time, responsibility for failure and reward for success are unequivocally ascribed to individuals or their partnerships. There is no point in going into technicalities here; they are far from being convincingly elaborated, especially with respect to large enterprises.[15] However, the emergence of this concept is significant in itself as an indication of the direction and of the radicalism of the attempts to resolve the conflict between state ownership and entrepreneurship.

In sum, our brief survey of the possibilities of reshaping the state enterprise sector, widely discussed in the wake of the radicalization of economic reforms in countries of 'real socialism' at the end of the 1980s, suggests that the chances of bringing the behaviour of state enterprises closer to the requirements of an effective market mechanism are the greater the further such enterprises are removed from state ownership in the traditional sense. In addition, during the period mentioned above, the reformers have come increasingly to acknowledge the need for a domestic non-state environment to make state enterprises more like businesses. Competition on equal terms from private sector (cooperatives including) enterprises, especially in areas of high opportunities for product and process innovation, is seen as vital for kicking the state sector out of its habitual complacency and reliance on soft criteria, and even for breeding the new managerial skills indispensable under market conditions but mostly absent among those brought up in the old system. Taken jointly, these two points lead inexorably to the question: why insist on state ownership at all? What actually are the advantages of getting state enterprises to imitate the behaviour of private ones through enormous and by no means assuredly successful efforts, or of devising bewilderingly complex schemes to make individuals act as entrepreneurs without becoming owners? The original critics of market socialism have refuted the validity of similar ideas as artificial and ineffective.[16] Does our analysis throw a different light on the matter?

Under MS, several possible reasons for state ownership of enterprises might be advanced. The first is to obtain the revenues needed by the state to carry out its politico-administrative functions, to provide social security, human and material infrastructure, and so on—in short, to maintain the non-enterprise sector. However, MS as defined here allows the state to obtain revenue from state enterprises only in the form of taxes and charges for capital. Residual profit, particularly the reward for entrepreneurial success, belongs to the enterprise itself, except perhaps in Liska's 'entrepreneurial socialism', where some element of the state participation in entrepreneurial gains may emerge as a result of the increasing value of the consecutive bids. On the whole, though, there seems to be no reason why the revenue could not be collected by the state in a similar way from non-state enterprises. As for the amount of revenue, this would depend on comparative efficiency and the potential for payment evasion; the first factor can hardly be counted in favour of the state enterprise, the second perhaps slightly so but by no means strongly enough to tip the overall balance.

The second point to consider is the possible role of the state enterprise in macroeconomic intervention, particularly that described in Chapter 9 as 'planning for long-term full employment', as the countercyclical measures do not go beyond conventional monetary and fiscal policies. Would private (non-state) enterprise be an obstacle to such intervention, perhaps for reasons similar to those advanced by Kalecki in his seminal paper 'Political Aspects of Full Employment'[17]—the dislike of government investment and spending on consumption, the desire to brandish the stick of the 'disciplining effect' of unemployment at the workforce? Should this be the case, state enterprise might be regarded as creating a more favourable environment for long-term macroeconomic policies. But it seems hardly warranted to expect private enterprise under a socialist government committed to full employment to reach 'the privileged position business occupies in capitalist countries',[18] so the analogy would be rather far-fetched. What about the relation of state and private enterprise respectively to the possible methods of intervention? As suggested in Chapter 9, the main instrument of long-term state intervention may be the charge on assets used to effect appropriate adjustments in the macrodistribution of national income between profits and wages. It may be argued that levying a charge on assets and turning the proceeds into a source of infrastructural investment and of a dividend for all members of the society can be intellectually and politically justified when the assets are owned by the state as a representative of the society. The economically equivalent alternative—a type of wealth tax on private enterprise assets— would be devoid of such justification; moreover, it might be regarded as encroachment on private property rights and hence might generate political resistance, which public ownership would not. This argument deserves perhaps some attention, but it must be weighed against other factors, among them the probability that private enterprise might be more responsive than state enterprise to indirect methods of intervention. Then there is the question of how much political clout the private sector would possess to resist the capital charge—a point similar to that mentioned above, but particularly relevant for transitional processes from 'real socialism' to MS.

The third possible reason for insisting on state ownership under MS concerns the size distribution of income and wealth. It is thought that by keeping enterprises in public hands, income and wealth differentials can be held lower than in the private economy without weakening incentives. The point is as important as it is difficult to adjudicate. Among the things which have entered conventional wisdom in the course of the reform drive in countries of 'real socialism' is also the recognition of the need to allow the income and wealth differentials to widen for the sake of efficiency, and—in particular—for the sake of promoting entrepreneurship. Where lies the 'optimal' range, supposed to balance the incentive with the equity aspect, nobody can tell. A hardly reliable clue is to be found in the experience of the developed capitalist countries, which provide a highly diverse picture of wealth and income relativities, correlated not so much with differences in entrepreneurial qualities as with divergent cultures, varying degrees of tolerance to redistributive taxation, and so on. If we can include a country like Sweden into the capitalist category, a strong egalitarian streak in distribution must be acknowledged, stronger than in a number of countries of 'real socialism', but displaying no correlation whatsoever with public ownership of means of production. Nevertheless it may well be that, compared with capitalism as a whole, MS with state enterprise would manage to combine managerial and entrepreneurial incentives with greater moderation in income and wealth differentials. This may be particularly true with regard to the possibility of eliminating or at least curbing the extravagantly large rentier-type incomes and capital gains from pure ownership unrelated to economic activity and passed from generation to generation. However, two things must be remembered in this context: first, that MS must legitimize income from property and entrepreneurship along with 'distribution according to work'; and secondly, as MS seems hardly feasible in practice without a sizeable non-state sector competing with state enterprises on equal terms, state ownership cannot be the only factor determining distribution.

On balance, although the pure logic of the fully fledged market mechanism seems to indicate the non-state (private) enterprise as the more natural constituent of the enterprise sector, the case for state enterprise should not be regarded as inevitably lost. Apart from the points made above, one has to keep in mind that the subject of our discussion here is not the choice between abstract alternatives in an empty space, but the direction of evolution of 'real socialism'. The process unfolds from a position in which state enterprise dominates, and this fact of life cannot be changed overnight. Thus a mixed economy where various forms of state enterprise would gradually be made to compete on an equal footing with private firms and cooperatives seems the only realistic prospect for MS in the foreseeable future. This means that the question of whether state enterprise can be fitted into a genuine market framework, including the capital market, and if so how to do it with minimal losses, remains highly relevant.

As for the long-term perspective, the development of the ownership structure would have to be left to the unbiased test of socio-economic suitability in ever-changing circumstances. In other words, the requirement may not be that of absolute renunciation of public ownership but certainly that of renunciation of any sort of ownership doctrinairism. The economic system becomes open-ended.

Concluding Remarks

This short book, unlike some of our previous works, has not been intended to investigate a normative model of an economic system which ought to emerge from the process of reforming 'real socialism'. One of the reasons for this reticence lies in our experience of past such model-building, which—as mentioned a number of times in the preceding pages—in the end proved scarcely successful. We have come to share the view of those participants in the reform debates in communist countries who express doubts about the usefulness of efforts to define the ultimate model of the economic system.

The intention behind this book has been to study the process of actual evolution of 'real socialism', why this evolution displayed an increasingly stronger tendency towards market socialism (MS) proper, and what kinds of problem are involved in the realization of this tendency. The possible features of MS discussed in Chapter 9 and 10 are not prescriptive, and we have tried to refrain from passing verdicts on the viability of various reform proposals aimed at creating conditions thought propitious for subordination of the economy to market coordination. Among the repercussions of this self-limitation is also the omission of the problem of whether MS should be regarded as the only way for 'real socialism' to stand up to the economic challenge, or whether the alternative exists of making direct central planning workable, for instance (as some think) along East German lines. We have taken the market-oriented tendency as sufficiently important in historical scale to concentrate on bringing out its full implications.

These implications are not confined to particular issues or institutions. It should be clear from our discussion that the concept of MS introduces for us a new dimension to the socialism versus capitalism controversy which has dominated much of the world in the course of the last century. If socialism—in the most general terms—must include in its economic characteristics the dominance of public ownership, central planning, and distribution according to work, then market socialism proper obviously sins in more than one way against each of these pillars of faith, and quite a degree of sophistry would be required to declare it imperturbably as yet another version of a socialist economic system.

A cruel East European wisecrack defines socialism as 'the painful road to capitalism'. It may be too much, or at least premature, to see in MS simply a stage on this road (or slide, as many would say), but there is little doubt in our minds that the distinctions between capitalist and socialist economic systems, as hitherto perceived, become under MS thoroughly blurred. If therefore marketization is accepted as the cure for the economic ills of 'real socialism', not only the original Marxist promise has to be cast aside as anachronistic, but also the very concept of transition from capitalism to socialism. The evolution of 'real socialism' complements in this respect the reverse regularity discussed in Chapter 2: while advanced capitalism fails to display the expected propensity to transform itself into socialism, the more 'real socialism' matures the more it is compelled to borrow from the capitalist armoury. The recourse to MS means that socialism should actually cease to be perceived at all as a bounded system, transcending the institutional framework developed in the past, and hence by definition postulating its total replacement by new institutional foundations, if not immediately so then in a longer perspective. The recourse to MS means, on the contrary, that the very idea of the grand design of a supremely rational economy has been acknowledged as utterly fallacious, and that the true and most difficult problem now is how to restore the continuity broken by the revolution from which the 'real socialist' economy emerged.

Market socialism proper, insofar as it can be visualized in the trends already revealed, does not imply the abandonment of a number of basic socialist values—equality of opportunity, major concern for full employment, social care, and so on. In taking parts of the economy out of market coordination, in preserving a place of substance for macroeconomic policy, including what we have called long-term planning, the concept of MS shaping up towards the end of the century retains the belief in the existence of an overall interest of society which cannot just be reduced to a sum of individual self-interests. In this sense it is still exposed to criticism from the extreme liberal positions. Whether this criticism will prove correct—as has been after all the case with the Mises/Hayek type of charge against orthodox socialism—is, in our view, too early to say. However, what is appealing in the concept of market socialism proper—and at this point we do not refrain from taking sides—is its evident open-endedness, which may allow it to move along flexibly enough with pragmatically validated exigencies.

Notes

Chapter 1

1 Among the recent works, perhaps the most important is Alec Nove's, *The Economics of Feasible Socialism* (Allen & Unwin, London, 1983). As far as the older writings are concerned, the authors want to acknowledge an excellent survey of the Marxist theory of communist socio-economic formation by Gabriel Temkin, *Karola Marksa obraz gospodarki komunistycznej* (*Karl Marx's Image of the Communist Economy*), published in Polish (Warsaw, 1962).

2 Michael Harrington, 'Leisure as the Means of Production', in '*The Socialist Idea: A Reappraisal*, eds Leszek Kolakowski and Stuart Hampshire (Basic Books, New York, 1974), 161.

3 See Elisabeth Durbin, *New Jerusalems: The Labour Party and the Economics of Democratic Socialism*, foreword Roy Hattersley (Routledge & Kegan Paul, London, 1985).

4 See, for instance, Janos Kornai, 'Efficiency and the Principles of Socialist Ethics', in *Contradictions and Dilemmas: Studies on the Socialist Economy and Society*, in English (Corvina, Budapest, 1983).

5 Włodzimierz Brus, *Socialist Ownership and Political Systems* (Routledge & Kegan Paul, London, 1975).

6 Oskar Lange, *Political Economy*, vol. I, ch. 5, English edn (Pergamon, Oxford, 1963).

7 Friedrich Engels, *Anti-Dühring: Herr Eugen Dühring's Revolution in Science*, English trans. from the 3rd German edn, 1894. (Lawrence & Wishart, London, 1969).

8 Brus, *Socialist Ownership*, ch. 2, section 3.

9 Karl Marx, *Capital: A Critique of Political Economy*, ed. F. Engels, vol. III, ch. XV, section III, English edition (Foreign Languages Publishing House, Moscow, 1962), 250–3.

10 Michał Kalecki, 'Theories of Growth in Different Social Systems', *Scientia* CV (May–June 1970), 21.

11 Joseph A. Schumpeter, *Capitalism, Socialism and Democracy*, 5th edn with a new introduction by Tom Bottomore (Allen & Unwin, London, 1976), 194.

12 Harvey Leibenstein, 'Microeconomics and X-Efficiency Theory', in *The*

Crisis in Economic Theory eds D. Bell and I. Kristol (Basic Books, New York, 1981), 98.

13 Karl Marx, 'Preface' to 'A Contribution to the Critique of Political Economy', in K. Marx and F. Engels *Selected Works in Two Volumes*, vol. I (Lawrence & Wishart, London, 1950), 329.

14 Schumpeter, *Capitalism, Socialism and Democracy*, 219.

Chapter 2

1 Joan Robinson, 'Marx, Marshall and Keynes', in *Collected Economic Papers*, vol. 2 (Basil Blackwell, Oxford, 1960), 15.

2 This assertion was made by Brus, *Socialist Ownership*, 13.

3 Characteristic of this kind of discussion is *Market Socialism: Whose Choice? A Debate*, Fabian Society pamphlet 516 (London, 1986).

Chapter 3

1 Vladimir I. Lenin, 'O nashey revolutsii' ('On Our Revolution'), in *Sochinenya (Works)*, 5th ed, vol. 45 (Moscow, 1964), 378.

2 A succinct presentation of Soviet development strategy can be found in Alec Nove, *An Economic History of the USSR* (Allen Lane & Penguin, London, 1969). Alexander Erlich, *The Soviet Industrialization Debate 1924–1928* (Harvard University Press, Cambridge, Mass., 1960) still gives the best account of the theoretical and political controversies in the process of working out the strategy. The present authors also acknowledge Gregory Grossman's overall assessment of Soviet development strategy in a historical context: 'Economics of Virtuous Haste: A View of Soviet Industrialization and Institutions', in *Marxism, Central Planning, and the Soviet Economy: Economic Essays in Honor of Alexander Erlich*, ed. Padma Desai (MIT Press, Cambridge, Mass., 1983).

3 See Michał Kalecki, *Introduction to the Theory of Growth in a Socialist Economy*, English edn (Basil Blackwell, Oxford, 1969).

4 Yosif V. Stalin, 'Ryeĉ na predvibornom sobranii izbirateley Stalinskogo okruga goroda Moskvy 9 Fevralya 1946 g.' ('Speech at the Pre-electoral Meeting in the Stalin Electoral Precinct of Moscow 9 February 1946,), in Works, vol. 3 (XVI) (Hoover Institution, Stanford, Calif., 1967), 14–15.

5 Maurice Dobb, *An Essay on Growth and Planning* (Routledge & Kegan Paul, London, 1960); Amartya K. Sen, *Choice of Techniques* (Basil Blackwell, Oxford, 1960).

6 For the USSR see for example Abram Bergson, *The Real National Income of Soviet Russia since 1928* (Harvard University Press, Cambridge, Mass., 1961); Abram Bergson and Simon Kuznets (eds), *Economic Trends in the*

Soviet Union (Harvard University Press, Cambridge, Mass., 1963); Rush Greenslade, 'The Real Gross National Product of the USSR, 1950–1975', in *Soviet Economy in a New Perspective*, Joint Economic Committee (US Government Printing Office, Washington, 1976); and Laurie Kurtzweg, 'Trends in Soviet Gross National Product', in *Gorbachev's Economic Plans*, Joint Economic Committee, US Government Printing Office, Washington, 1987). The growth of Eastern European countries is analysed by: Thad P. Alton, 'East European GNPs: Origin of Product, Final Uses, Rates of Growth, and International Comparison', in *Slow Growth in the 1980s*, Joint Economic Committee (US Government Printing Office, Washington, 1985); Thad P. Alton, 'Comparison of Overall Economic Performance in the East European Countries', NATO Economic Colloqium, Brussels, 1988; Peter Havlik and Friedrich Levcik, 'GDP of Czechoslovakia, 1970–1980', study prepared for the Second Workshop on CPE National Income Statistics, World Bank Staff Working Paper 772, The World Bank, Washington, 1985, and Stanislaw Gomulka, 'Industrialisation and the Rate of Growth: Eastern Europe 1955–75', in *Growth, Innovation and Reform in Eastern Europe* (Wheatsheaf, Brighton, 1986).

7 According to Western estimates the (average annual) rate of growth of Soviet GNP amounted to 5.1 per cent in the years 1929–40, 2.1 per cent 1941–50, 5.2 per cent 1951–75, and 2.1 per cent 1976–85. Hence the average for the whole period 1929–85 was 4.1 per cent, or 4.5 per cent if the untypical years between 1940 and 1950 are excluded. Both rates exceed the century growth rates of all major capitalist countries except Japan. If, however, the analysis is limited to the period 1951–85 the rate of growth of Soviet GNP amounts still to 4.2 per cent but does not differ substantially from the average growth rates of industrialized capitalist countries. Indeed the latter group, contrary to the economic stagnation of the 1930s, accelerated their growth substantially in the postwar era. See Paul R. Gregory, 'Economic Growth and Structural Change in Czarist Russia and the Soviet Union: A Long-Term Comparison', in *Economic Welfare and the Economics of Soviet Socialism: Essays in Honor of Abram Bergson*, ed. Steven Rosefielde (Cambridge University Press, Cambridge, 1981); Paul R. Gregory and Robert C. Stuart, *Soviet Economic Structure and Performance*, 3rd edn (Harper and Row, New York, 1986); and Kurtzweg, 'Trends in Soviet Gross National Product'. It is worthwhile mentioning that official Soviet growth rates of aggregated output are now being criticized inside the USSR itself. This criticism not only supports Western estimates but sometimes goes further in the revision of Soviet official data. Thus the growth rate for the years 1929–85 has been calculated at the level of 3.2–3.5 per cent, almost one percentage point below the growth rate of 4.1 per cent given above. See Boris Bolotin, 'Sovetsky Sojuz w mirowoi ekonomike, 1917–1987' ('The Soviet Union

and World Economy, 1917–1987'), *Mirovaya Ekonomika i mezhdunarodnye Otnosheniya (MEMO)* no. 11, (November 1987), cited in Anders Aslund, 'How Small is the Soviet National Income?', paper presented at the Hoover-Rand Conference at Stanford University, 23–4 March 1988, Kennan Institute, Washington; and especially the famous article of Vasily Selyunin and Grigory Khanin, 'Lukavaya tsifra' ('The Cunning Figure'), *Novyi mir* 63 (2) (1987).

8 Laski and Askanas have found that the official (average annual) rate of growth of private consumption in Poland in the years 1965–78 (5.4 per cent) should be cut by about two percentage points because of the unreported price inflation: Benedykt Askanas and Kazimierz Laski, 'Consumer Prices and Private Consumption in Poland and Austria', *Journal of Comparative Economics* no. 9 (1985). Havlik and Levcik have come to the conclusion that the rate of growth of GNP in Czechoslovakia in the years 1971–80 was 1.7 per cent, against the official figure (although of net material product) of 4.7 per cent: Havlik and Levcik, 'GDP of Czechoslovakia', 33 and 37. According to Alton the rates of growth in the period 1966–80 were: in Bulgaria 5.3 per cent (against the official 7.5 per cent); in Czechoslovakia 4.5 per cent (5.4 per cent); in DDR 4.5 per cent (4.9 per cent); in Hungary 4.2 per cent (5.4 per cent); in Poland 5.6 per cent (5.7 per cent); and in Romania 7.9 per cent (8.7 per cent). In his view the inflation of official growth rates persists, although it is much smaller: Alton, 'East European GNPs', 109–10. See also *Comecon Data 1985*, ed. Vienna Institute for Comparative Economic Studies (Macmillan Press, 1986), 50.

9 According to CIA assessment, Soviet GNP per caput, converted at USA purchasing power equivalents, amounted in 1985 to about 50 per cent of the USA level: CIA *Handbook of Economic Statistics 1986* (Washington, 1986). Aslund comes to the conclusion that this estimate should be halved and that the USSR has not advanced economically in relation to the USA since 1928: Aslund, 'How Small is the Soviet National Income?'. It should be stressed that according to the International Comparison Project (ICP) Hungary's GDP per caput in 1985 amounted to 31.2 per cent of the USA level. If both the CIA and ICP estimates are true, then the aggregate output per caput would be about 60 per cent higher in the USSR than in Hungary. It is, however, generally admitted that the aggregated output per caput in both countries is rather similar. *Purchasing Power Parities and Real Expenditures* (OECD, 1985); *International Comparison of Gross Domestic Product in Europe 1985*, (United Nations, in print). See, too, Peter Havlik, *Comparison of Real Products between East and West, 1970–1983*, Forschungsbericht 115, Vienna Institute for Comparative Economic Studies, April 1986; Irving B. Kravis, Alan Heston, and Robert Summers, *World Product and Income: International Comparisons of Real Gross Product* (Johns Hopkins University Press for the World Bank,

Baltimore and London, 1982); Paul Marer, *Dollar GNPs of the USSR and Eastern Europe* (Johns Hopkins University Press, Baltimore, 1985); and Robert Summers and Alan Heston, 'A New Set of International Comparisons of Real Product and Price Levels Estimates for 130 Countries, 1950–1985', *Review of Income and Wealth*, no. 2, June 1984.

10 This can be illustrated with data on the growth of GNP and factor inputs (average annual growth rates) in the USSR in 1961–85 (Kurtzweg, 'Trends in Soviet Gross National Product,' 134–5):

Years	GNP	Factor inputs*			Factor productivity**
		Labour	Capital	Combined	
1961–65	4.8	1.5	8.8	4.5	0.3
1966–70	5.1	2.0	7.4	4.2	0.8
1971–75	3.0	1.7	8.0	4.3	−1.3
1976–80	2.3	1.2	6.9	3.6	−1.2
1981–85	1.9	0.7	6.2	3.0	−1.0

* Disregarding land.
** Growth rate of GNP minus growth rate of combined inputs.

Starting from 1971 the total factor productivity decreased. If the whole period 1928–85 (except the years 1941–50) is considered, total factor productivity in the USSR has increased. With the average annual growth rates for output, labour, and capital at about 5.2, 2, and 8 per cent respectively, the combined factor inputs grew at about 3.8 per cent and factor productivity at about 1.4 per cent. According to this calculation the growth of inputs accounted for about three-quarters of output growth and the growth of factor productivity for only one-quarter. In the industrialized capitalist countries, for the same period, the growth of factor productivity accounted for about two-thirds of output growth: Gregory, 'Economic Growth and Structural Change', 45–6.

11 The term was used in Włodzimierz Brus and Tadeusz Kowalik, 'Socialism and Development', *Cambridge Journal of Economics*, no. 7 (1983).

12 The Soviet formula, adopted at the XXVIIth Congress of the CPSU in the so-called 'new edition' of the programme of the party, states literally that 'our country has *entered* the stage of developed socialism.'

13 Janos Kornai, *Economics of Shortage*, English edn (North-Holland, Amsterdam, New York, Oxford, 1980).

Chapter 4

1 Vladimir I. Lenin, 'K Četiryohletney godovschchine Oktyabrskoy Revolutsii' ('On the Fourth Anniversary of the October Revolution'), *Works*, vol. 44, 151.

2 Włodzimierz Brus, *Ogolne problemy funkcjonowania gospodarki socjalistycznej* (*General Problems of Functioning of a Socialist Economy*) (Warsaw, 1961). The

term 'centralistic' was meant to emphasize the difference between on the one hand the excessive and bureaucratic centralization of the command economy, and on the other the system of central planning as such which the author then regarded as compatible with the regulated market mechanism. Unfortunately, in the English edition 'centralistic' was rejected in favour of 'centralized', which blurred the intended differentiation: *The Market in a Socialist Economy* (London, Boston, 1972).

3 The point about the role of ideological factors was made forcefully by Richard Löwenthal in his seminal paper 'Development versus Utopia in Communist Policy', in *Change in Communist Systems,* ed. Chalmers Johnson (Stanford, 1970).

4 The designation 'coercive model' was introduced by Michael Ellman, *Socialist Planning* (Cambridge, 1979) to describe the way resources for the rapid industrialization of the USSR were obtained from agriculture. We use it here in a broader sense.

5 The term is from Kornai, *Economics of Shortage.*

6 These implications of the command system are discussed in a number of Laski's papers, especially in 'Wirtschaftsreformen in Osteuropa als Gegenstand der Wirtschaftstheorie' ('Economic Reforms in Eastern Europe as a Subject of Economic Theory'), in *Vierteljahrshefte zur Wirtschaftsforschung,* Heft 2 (Deutsches Institut fur Wirtschaftsforschung, Berlin, 1985); and 'Marx-Sozialismus, Markt-Sozialismus und Wirtschaftsreformen des "real existierenden Sozialismus"' ('Marxist Socialism, Market Socialism, and Economic Reforms in "Really Existing Socialism"'), in *Forschungsberichte,* Vienna Institute for Comparative Economic Studies, no. 129, June 1987.

7 The term 'planning paradox' is used by Ruud Knaack in 'Comparative Economics: Lessons from Socialist Planning', in *Comparative Economic Systems—Present Views,* ed. A. Zimbalist (Kluwer-Nijhoff, Boston, 1984).

8 This point is made by David Granick, 'Central Physical Planning, Incentives and Job Rights', in *'Comparative Economic Systems—Present Views.*

9 Cezary Józefiak, 'Traditional Central Planning and Evolutionary Trends', in *Contributions to East-European Economic Research,* Netherlands Economic Institute, no. 3, 1983.

10 We follow here the classification given by Gregory and Stuart, *Soviet Economic Structure and Performance,* 219–21.

Chapter 5

1 The clearest general statement presenting the Marxist-Leninist position on the relationship beween socialism and the market is probably to be found in the *Programme of the Communist International* adopted at its VIth Congress in 1928, ch. 4, English edn (London, 1929), 31–3. See in this

context W. Brus, 'Utopianism and Realism in the Evolution of the Soviet Economic System', *Soviet Studies*, XL(3) (July 1988).

2 A brief discussion of their views is included in the historical survey (ch. 2) of Brus, *The Market in a Socialist Economy*.

3 The literature directly or indirectly connected with the debate on market socialism or economic calculation under socialism is enormous and growing. Therefore, instead of trying to compile a more or less representative general list here, it seems more expedient to direct the interested reader to what the authors regard as the most comprehensive index of books and articles on the subject, available in the important book by Don Lavoie, *Rivalry and Central Planning: The Socialist Calculation Debate Reconsidered* (Cambridge University Press, Cambridge, 1985). Needless to say, we shall refer to particular works when discussing specific issues. Lerner's rule is: if the value of the marginal (physical) product of any factor is greater than the price of the factor, increase output; if less, reduce output; if equal, maintain output; A. Lerner, *The Economics of Control* (Macmillan, New York, 1944), 64.

4 Oskar Lange, 'Marxian Economics and Modern Economic Theory', *Review of Economic Studies* (June 1935), reprinted in *Essential Works of Socialism*, ed. Irving Howe (Holt, Rinehart, & Winston, New York, Chicago, San Francisco, 1970), 343–56.

5 Abram Bergson, 'Socialist Economics', in *A Survey of Contemporary Economics*, ed. Howard S. Ellis, vol. 1 (Irwin, Homewood, Ill. 1949).

6 Leon Walras, *Elements of Pure Economics* (Irwin, Homewood, Ill., 1954).

7 This point was made by James E. Meade, *The Stationary Economy: Principles of Political Economy* (Unwin, London, 1966), chs. XIII–XV.

8 Benjamin N. Ward, *The Socialist Economy: A Study of Organizational Alternatives* (Random House, New York, 1967), 30–40.

9 Luigi L. Pasinetti, *Lectures on the Theory of Production* (Columbia University Press, New York, 1977), 24–32 and 183–4.

10 Those who never subscribed to such optimistic assumptions strike hard at the neglect of examining the motivational aspects of the Lange-Lerner model, as for example, James M. Buchanan: 'We may well ask why economists did not stop to ask the question why socialist managers would behave in terms of the idealized rules. Where are the economic eunuchs to be found to operate the system?'; *Liberty, Market and the State: Political Economy in the 1980s* (Wheatsheaf, Brighton, 1986), 25.

11 This is particularly true of Lavoie, *Rivalry and Central Planning*. Moreover, from the point of view of the general subject of the present book it is significant that similar conclusions are reached by those authors who return to the calculation debate in the context of economic reforms in countries of 'real socialism'. The section on the theoretical aspects of the reform designs in the admirable survey by Janos Kornai, 'The Hungarian Reform Process: Visions, Hopes and Reality', *Journal of Economic Literature*

(December 1986), provides a good case in point. Another attempt of this kind, namely Gabriel Temkin, 'On Economic Reforms in Socialist Countries: The Debate on Economic Calculation Under Socialism Revisited' (*Communist Economics*, vol. I, no. 1, 1989), amounts actually to a full vindication of the Mises/Hayek position.

12 Lavoie, *Rivalry and Central Planning*, 104–11.

13 Kornai, 'The Hungarian Reform Process', 1727.

14 The weakness of Lange's model in a situation of conflict between the current equilibrium conditions and the exigencies of rapid structural changes was asserted by Maurice Dobb, 'A Note on Saving and Investment in a Socialist Economy', *Economic Journal* (December 1939). Paul A. Baran developed a similar argument in his essay 'National Economic Planning. Part 3: Planning under Socialism' in *A Survey of Contemporary Economics*, ed. B. Haley, vol. 2 (Irwin, Homewood, Ill., 1952). Paul M. Sweezy used the Yugoslav example in an attempt to show the incompatibility of the market with a socialist economy in 'The Transition from Socialism to Capitalism?', *Monthly Review* 16 (1964).

15 The text of the preface is published in vol. 2 of the *Collected Works* of Oskar Lange, in Polish: Oskar Lange, *Dzieła*, tom 2 (Warszawa, 1973). In the same volume is printed the letter to F. A. Hayek (of 31 August 1940, in response to the receipt of Hayek's paper 'Socialist Calculation: The Competitive Solution') which contains the following passage: 'I hope you will not mind if I allow myself to characterize your position as the passage to the third line of defence; this time you move the weight of the argument from pure static aspects to the dynamic ones. In doing so, however, you move the whole question exactly on the level, which is indeed important but requires—before a satisfactory answer can be found—new research and explanations; there is no question that you have succeeded in raising essential problems and in showing gaps in the pure static solution given by me. I intend to work on this subject and to give an answer to your paper . . . sometime in the fall'; *Dzieła*, 567. Despite the fact that Lange never fulfilled this promise, he maintained in the article 'The Computer and the Market', written a few months before his death in 1965, that 'in my essay [the 1936–7 one] I refuted the Hayek-Robbins argument by showing how a market mechanism could be established in a socialist economy which would lead to the solution of the simultaneous equations by means of an empirical procedure of trial and error.' Without mentioning Hayek's argument, he apparently viewed the questions pertaining to the market as of a static nature only, whereas dynamic problems are to be solved under socialism by another mechanism: 'For planning economic development, long-term investments have to be taken out of the market mechanism and based on the judgement of developmental economic policy' helped by the use of the 'electronic computer which [here] does not replace the market. It fulfils a function

which the market never was able to perform'; Oskar Lange, 'The Computer and the Market', in *Capitalism, Socialism and Economic Growth: Essays in Honour of Maurice H. Dobb'* ed. C. Feinstein, (Cambridge 1967) 158–61.

Chapter 6

1 *Programme of the League of Communists of Yugoslavia* (*Program Saveza Komunista Jugoslavije*) (Kultura, Beograd, 1958). This document, adopted at the VIIth Congress of the LCY, is probably the best exposition of the 'Yugoslav way to socialism'. It is known as the 'Ljubljana programme' from the name of the city where the Congress was held.
2 See Włodzimierz Brus, 'The East European Economic Reforms: What Happened To Them?', *Soviet Studies* XXXI (2) (1979).
3 David Granick, *Enterprise Guidance in Eastern Europe: A Comparison of Four Socialist Economies* (Princeton, 1975), 305.
4 The principles of the Hungarian reform of 1968 which created the so-called New Economic Mechanism were presented in English by the contributors to the design themselves in a volume edited by Istvan Friss, *Reform of the Economic Mechanism in Hungary* (Publishing House of the Hungarian Academy of Sciences, Budapest, 1969). They can also be found in Granick, *Enterprise Guidance*, part III, as well as in Paul Hare, Hugo Radice, and Nigel Swain (eds), *Hungary: A Decade of Economic Reform* (Allen & Unwin, Hemel Hempstead, 1981). One of the present authors (W. Brus) discusses the main features of the Hungarian reform of 1968 in ch. 26 of *The Economic History of Eastern Europe 1919–1975*, vol. III, *Institutional Change within a Planned Economy'*, ed. M. C. Kaser (Clarendon Press, Oxford, 1986). An interesting attempt to discuss the Hungarian reform in more general terms of economics of socialism is presented by Jean-Charles Asselain, *Planning and Profits in Socialist Economies*, English trans. (Routledge & Kegan Paul, London, 1984).
5 Statistical data are based on official national publications, mostly as tabulated in the periodical surveys of economic performance by the Vienna Institute for Comparative Economic Studies.
6 Kornai, 'The Hungarian Reform Process'.
7 Ibid.
8 Ibid, 1699–700.
9 Ibid, 1697, 1719.
10 The first account of the reappearance of 'storming' under the NEM was published by M. Laki, 'End-Year Rush-Work in Hungarian Industry and Foreign Trade', *Acta Oeconomica* 25 (1–2) (1980). A further analysis in a comparative context was provided by Jacek Rostowski and Paul Auerbach, 'Storming Cycles and Economic Systems'. *Journal of Comparative Economics* 10 (3) (September 1986).

11 Granick, *Enterprise Guidance*.
12 Ibid., 10.
13 Kornai, *Economics of Shortage'*, ch. 22, 'The Degrees of Paternalism'.
14 The point is stressed with particular emphasis by M. Tardos, 'The Conditions of Developing a Regulated Market', *Acta Oeconomica* 36 (1–2) (1986); we return to Tardos's argument in the next chapter. See also in the same issue of *Acta Oeconomica* the article by L. Szamuelyi, 'Prospects of Economic Reforms in the CMEA Countries in the '8os'.

Chapter 7

1 *Anti-Dühring*, 370.
2 Oskar Lange, 'On the Economic Theory of a Socialist Economy', in *On the Economic Theory of Socialism'*, Oskar Lange and Fred Taylor (Lippincott ed., Minneapolis, 1938); paperback edn (McCraw-Hill, New York, 1964), 85.
3 Lerner, *The Economics of Control*, 263 and 314–15.
4 Lange, 'On the Economic Theory'.
5 Dobb, 'A Note on Savings and Investment'.
6 Baran, 'National Economic Planning'.
7 Michał Kalecki, *Theory of Economic Dynamics*, revised second edn (Allen & Unwin, 1965; published in America by Monthly Review Press, 1968), 50 and 73.
8 See Michał Kalecki, 'The Scope of the Evaluation of the Efficiency of Investment in a Socialist Economy', in *Selected Essays on the Economic Growth of the Socialist and the Mixed Economy* (Cambridge University Press, Cambridge, 1972).
9 An examination of East European economic reforms *inter alia* from this point of view can be found in chs 25 and 26 of vol. III of *The Economic History of Eastern Europe 1919–1975*.
10 Sun Ye-fang, *Some Theoretical Problems in the Socialist Economy* in Chinese, (Beijing, 1979), as reviewed by C. Lin in *China Quarterly* no. 98 (June 1984), 357–61.
11 This is the model developed in Brus, *The Market in a Socialist Economy*.
12 Istvan Friss (ed.), *Reform of the Economic Mechanism in Hungary*.
13 Ibid., 73.
14 Ibid., 19–20.
15 Ibid., 20.
16 Ibid., 17.
17 Ibid., 16.
18 Ibid.
19 Schumpeter, *Capitalism, Socialism and Democracy*, 81–6.
20 Granick, *Enterprise Guidance*, 281.
21 Tardos, 'The Conditions of Developing a Regulated Market'.
22 Ibid., 83.

Chapter 8

1 The formulation is that of Jože Mencinger, 'The Yugoslav Economic Systems and Their Efficiency', *Economic Analysis and Workers' Management* XX (1) (1986). The author dates the 'mixed administrative cum self-management economy' as lasting from 1953 to 1962, and the 'labour-managed market economy' from 1963 to 1973. Other Yugoslav authors, as well as foreign scholars such as Harold Lydall, *Yugoslav Socialism: Theory and Practice* (Clarendon Press, Oxford, 1984), use different terminology and slightly different time dimensions, but their characterization of the changes in the Yugoslav economic system is basically similar to that of Mencinger, especially with regard to the significance of the reforms in the early 1960s.

2 For a comparative discussion of the two models see Brus, *Socialist Ownership and Political Systems*, ch. 2.

3 World Bank, *Yugoslavia: Development with Decentralization*, Report of a mission sent to Yugoslavia by the World Bank (Johns Hopkins University Press, Baltimore, 1975), 219.

4 Figures from World Bank, *Yugoslavia*, 221, Table 9.11.

5 Branko Horvat, 'Yugoslav Economic Policy in the Post-War Period: Problems, Ideas, Institutional Developments', *American Economic Review* LXI (3) (June 1971), part 2 supplement, 139.

6 Laura d'Andrea Tyson, 'Investment Allocation: A Comparison of the Reform Experiences in Hungary and Yugoslavia', *Journal of Comparative Economics* 7 (3) (1983), 296.

7 Granick, *Enterprise Guidance*, 342 and 468; Alexandar Bajt, 'Yugoslav Economic Reforms, Monetary and Production Mechanism', *Economics of Planning* VII (3) (1967).

8 Lydall, *Yugoslav Socialism*, 150.

9 Mencinger, 'The Yugoslav Economic Systems'. op. cit.

10 Zoran Pjaniĉ in the remarkable debate on 'All Our Reforms' in the Yugoslav magazine *Gledišta (Views)* (May–June 1986).

11 World Bank, *Yugoslavia*, 289.

12 Among others by Alexandar Bajt, 'Trideset godina privrednog rasta: problemi efikasnosti i društvenih odnosa' (Thirty Years of Economic Growth: Problems of Efficiency and Social Relations'), *Ekonomist* XXXVIII (1) (1985).

13 Kosta Mihailoviĉ, *Ekonomska Stvarnost Jugoslavije (The Economic Reality of Yugoslavia)*, 2nd edn (Beograd, 1982), 205.

14 Bajt 'Trideset godina privrednog rasta', 14.

15 The debate was conducted over several issues of *Gledišta* in 1986.

16 This point was made by France Černe in the May-June 1986 issue of *Gledišta*.

17 Tyson, 'Investment Allocation', 297.

18 Lydall, *Yugoslav Socialism*, 272. The entire ch. 13 of the book is devoted to the private sector.

19 Benjamin M. Ward, 'The Firm in Illyria', *American Economic Review*, 48 (September 1958). The article gave rise to a wide and still continuing debate on the behaviour of a labour-managed enterprise in comparison with a capitalist firm on the one hand and a state-owned socialist firm on the other. Chapter 3 of Lydall, *Yugoslav Socialism*, contains a useful survey of the debate and a statement of the author's own position. Some implications of this debate for the problem of ownership will be taken up in ch. 10 in this book.

20 Branko Horvat, 'Farewell to the Illyrian Firm'; Lubomir Madjar, 'The Illyrian Firm—An Alternative View'; Branko Horvat, 'The Illyrian Firm—An Alternative View: A Rejoinder'; *Economic Analysis and Workers' Management*, nos 1 and 4 (1986).

21 Erik G. Furubotn and Svetozar Pejoviĉ, 'Property Rights and the Behaviour of the Firm in a Socialist State: The Example of Yugoslavia', *Zeitschrift für Nationalökonomie*, (3–4) (1970).

22 Most prominent among Yugoslav economists in this respect is Branko Horvat.

23 Sofija Popov, 'Utvrdẑenje ličnih dohodaka u samoupravnom socijalizmu' (Determination of Personal Incomes in Self-Management Socialism'), *Ekonomska Misao*, no. 3 (September 1985).

24 The need to counteract under market socialism the danger of unemployment and excessive income differentials due to this kind of 'closed doors' tendency was acknowledged in 1934 by Oskar Lange and Marek Breit, who in their contribution to a programmatic document of one of the left-wing groupings of the Polish Socialist Party advanced a proposal by which self-managed enterprises 'are under obligation to employ all workers who apply for [work]'. For a comprehensive theoretical discussion of such a model and its implications see Alberto Chilosi, 'Self-Managed Socialism with "Free Mobility of Labour"', *Journal of Comparative Economics*, 10 (3) (1986).

25 Popov, 'Utrvdẑenje ličnih dohodaka u samoupravnom socijalizmu'.

Chapter 9

1 The absence of commercial banking may have been the very source of the relative success of issuance of bonds which provided at least some flexibility both for savers and for borrowers; on the other hand, the closed doors to the stock market acted in the same direction. This may help to explain the unusual popularity (in relative terms) of fixed interest bonds issued by enterprises.

2 The matter was first raised in Hungary in connection with the article by

Tibor Liska, 'Kritik es koncepcio: tezisek a gazdasagi reformiahoz' (Critique and Conception: Theses for a Reform of the Economic Mechanism), *Közgazdasagi Szemle*, no. 9 (1963). Dormant for a long period, Liska's ideas made a comeback in the 1980s, contributing to the wide recognition of the relevance of the joint stock company as a possible organizational pattern for state enterprises. It should be stressed however that Liska's 'entrepreneurial socialism' cannot be reduced to the market in equity shares; it is a different concept (see note 14 in Chapter 10). Examples of Polish publications on the subject are: Maciej Iwanek and Marcin Święcicki, 'Handlować kapitałem' ('Trading in capital'), *Polityka*, no. 24 (1987), and 'Socialist Joint-Stock Company: the Missing Link in Economic Reform', presented at the workshop on Financial Reform in Socialist Economies, European University Institute, Florence, 12–16 October 1987; Jacek A. Likowski, 'Droga przez giełdę' ('The way leads through the stock exchange') Supplement to *Polityka*, no. 22 (1987). A comprehensive analysis of the theoretical aspects of the market mechanism and their implications for Poland, among other things with regard to the capital market, is provided by Adam Lipowski, *Mechanizm rynkowy w gospodarce polskiej (The Market Mechanism in the Polish Economy)* (Państwowe Wydawnictwo Naukowe, Warszawa, 1988). Problems of equity shares in Yugoslavia are discussed by Milica Uvaliĉ, *Shareholding in Yugoslav Theory and Practice*, EUI Working Paper no. 88/330, European University Institute, Florence. A survey of and a contribution to the discussion can be found in Domenico Mario Nuti, *Financial Innovation under Market Socialism*, EUI Working Paper no. 87/285, European University Institute, Florence.

3 Michał Kalecki, *Selected Essays on the Dynamics of the Capitalist Economy 1933–1970* (Cambridge University Press, Cambridge, 1971) 43–4. See also Michio Morishima, *The Economics of Industrial Society* (Cambridge University Press, Cambridge, 1984), 25–37.

4 Amit Bhaduri, *Macroeconomics: The Dynamics of Commodity Production* (Macmillan, London, 1986), 36–54.

5 Kalecki, *Selected Essays*, 62–3.

6 It should perhaps be mentioned that the expected price flexibility acts in a socialist economy in one direction only. If investment has to increase (in relation to national income) the necessary increases in the price/cost ratio are as a rule not realized because the state tries to avoid unpopular measures for which it is being made directly responsible. As a result hidden price increases and suppressed inflation are often given priority over open price changes. Thus hidden price increases and suppressed inflation are specific forms under which 'price flexibility' manifests itself in a CPE when the price/cost ratio has to increase.

7 Kornai, *Contradictions and Dilemmas*, 45.

8 Maurice Dobb, *On Economic Theory and Socialism* (Routledge & Kegan Paul, London, 1955), 41–5.

9 Kalecki, *Selected Essays*, 38–41.
10 See K. Laski, *The Rate of Growth and the Rate of Interest in the Socialist Economy* (Springer, Vienna, New York, 1972), 88–90.
11 Michał Kalecki, 'Full Employment by Stimulating Private Investment?', *Oxford Economic Papers* no. 7, March 1945, 85–7.
12 Kalecki, *Selected Essays*, 41–2.
13 This instrument could be tried also in a situation of investment bigger than AB. Reduction of the capital charge combined with reduction of spending from this source should reduce profits and negatively influence the propensity to invest. However, reduction in spending of the CPB should take into account the implications of lowering the share of the CPB's spending in national income.

Chapter 10

1 Brus, *Socialist Ownership*.
2 Vaclav Holešovsky, *Economic Systems: Analysis and Comparison* (International Student Edition, McGraw-Hill Kogakusha, Tokyo, 1977), ch. 3, 41.
3 We are aware of the passages from vol. III of *Das Kapital*, sometimes cited to show that Marx's views on ownership as the decisive factor of control are more ambiguous, but despite this we maintain that our proposition reflects the general lines of Marxist theory correctly.
4 (eds), Erik G. Furubotn and Svetozar Pejoviĉ *The Economics of Property Rights* (Ballinger, Cambridge, Mass., 1974). See also the quotation from Milton Friedman's article in Holešovsky, *Economic Systems*, 55.
5 V. V. Novozhilov, 'Problems of Cost–Benefit Analysis in Optimal Planning' in *Mathematical Studies in Economics & Statisics in the USSR & Eastern Europe: A Journal of Translations* V, (2–4), (1968–9), ch. 2, 36–37.
6 This aspect of public ownership on a national scale is aptly stressed by Leszek Balcerowicz, 'Remarks on the Concept of Ownership', *Oeconomica Polona, Journal of the Economic Committee of the Polish Academy of Sciences and of the Polish Economic Society*, no. 1 (1987).
7 Such a point was strongly made by Maurice Garner, 'Has Public Enterprise Failed?', Templeton College, The Oxford Centre for Management Studies, December 1987, unpublished paper.
8 Abram Bergson, 'Managerial Risks and Rewards in Public Enterprises', *Journal of Comparative Economics* 2 (3), (September 1978).
9 Friedrich A. Hayek, 'Sozialistische Wirtschaftsrechnung III: Wiedereinfuhrung des Wettbewerbs' ('Socialist Economic Calculus III: The Reintroduction of Competition'), in *'Individualismus und wirtschaftliche Ordnung (Individualism and Economic Order)* (Erlenbach, Zurich, 1952). This point was reiterated with great emphasis by G. Warren Nutter, 'Markets Without Property: A Grand Illusion', in Furobotn and Pejoviĉ, *The*

Economics of Property Rights', as well as by the Polish sociologist Jadwiga Staniszkis in a number of articles published in the early 1980s and in her book *The Ontology of Socialism* (Oxford University Press, forthcoming). In a comparative perspective the problem is discussed comprehensively by Helmut Leipold, *Wirtschafts- und Gesellchafts-systeme im Vergleich (Economic and Social Systems in Comparison)*, 5th edn (Gustav Fischer, Stuttgart, 1988).

10 We have in mind here the ideas of Burnham himself, as in James Burnham, *The Managerial Revolution* (first published 1944), as well as of the pioneering work by A. A. Berle Jr and G. C. Means, *The Modern Corporation and Private Property* (1952) or of J. K. Galbraith, *The New Industrial State* (1968).

11 This has clearly been the case in Hungary at the beginning of the 1980s. See in particular T. Sárközy, 'Problems of Social Ownership and of Proprietory Organization', and M. Tardos, 'Development Program for Economic Control and Organization in Hungary', *Acta Oeconomica* 29 and 28 (1982) respectively. In the Polish literature the most comprehensive treatment of the subject known to us is that by Marek Dąbrowski, 'Podmiot przedsiębiorczości w róznych wariantach reform gospodarczych' (The Subject of Entrepreneurship in Different Variants of Economic Reforms'), *Ekonomista*, 3–4 (1988).

12 Harold Lydall, *Yugoslavia in Crisis* (Oxford University Press, 1989), regards this as one of the underlying causes of the crisis of the Yugoslav version of socialism (ch. 5).

13 M. S. Gorbachev, 'Speech to the 4th All-Union Congress of the Kolkhoz members', *Pravda* 24 March 1988.

14 The writings of Tibor Liska are not well known in the West, and in Hungary itself only the rather secondary or preliminary ones have been published. His apparently main exposition of 'entrepreneurial socialism', a book entitled *Econostat*, was circulated in mimeographed form. The most comprehensive presentation of Liska's ideas known to us is an article by J. Bársony, 'Tibor Liska's Concept of Socialist Entrepreneurship', *Acta Oeconomica* 28 (3–4) (1982), 422–55. In the same issue Janos Kornai comments on Liska's concept. Tibor Liska's ideas were also presented by Istvan Siklaky to the conference on Alternative Models of Socialist Economic Systems, Györ, Hungary, March 1988.

15 Evidence that in practice any implementation of Liska's ideas has been contemplated in Hungary exclusively with regard to small and medium enterprises may be found in J. Bársony and I. Siklaky, 'Some Reflections on Socialist Entrepreneurship', *Acta Oeconomica* 34 (1–2), 51–64.

16 Most explicit in this respect has been Ludwig von Mises. Disputing the coherence of the 'quasi-market' theories of Lange and Dickinson, Mises attacked forcefully the imitative design: 'They want to abolish private

control of the means of production, market exchange, market prices and competition. But at the same time they want to organize the socialist utopia in such a way that people could act *as if* these things were still present. They want people to play market as children play war, railroad, or school. They do not comprehend how such childish play differs from the real thing it tries to imitate'; *Human Action: A Treatise on Economics* (William Hodge, London, 1949), 706–7. Our attention has been drawn to this passage and similar others both by Mises and by Hayek by G. Temkin, 'On Economic Reforms in Socialist Countries'.

17 Michał Kalecki, 'Political Aspects of Full Employment', *Political Quarterly* XIV (4) (1953), 322–31.

18 Charles E. Lindblom, *Politics and Markets: The World's Political-Economic Systems* (Basic Books, New York, 1977), ch 13.

Index